Stay. Come. Heel.
Every Time.

The Warren Method of Dog Training
Using Love, Trust, and Respect

Kyle Warren

1st WORLD
PUBLISHING

Stay. Come. Heel. Every Time

The Warren Method of Dog Training Using Love, Trust, and Respect

Kyle Warren

Published by 1stWorld Publishing
1100 North 4th St. Suite 131, Fairfield, Iowa 52556
tel: 641-209-5000 • fax: 641-209-3001
web: www.1stworldpublishing.com

First Edition

LCCN: 2005911402
SoftCover ISBN: 1-59540-934-3
HardCover ISBN: 1-59540-980-7
eBook ISBN: 1-59540-979-3

Canine Instinct

CANINE COMMUNICATION

Basic & Advanced Skills
Aggression Rehab
Water, Upland, & Tracking Training

KYLE WARREN *Owner/Trainer*

845.399.3439
www.kylewarrendogs.com

Table of Contents

Introduction

The stage was set. It was a perfect day, cool, with a light breeze and dew on the grass. I was testing my six-month-old Hungarian Wirehaired Vizsla, Hazel, for the first time in NAVHDA (North American Versatile Hunting Dog Association). Despite her age, Hazel had been well prepared for this test. She had been tracking, swimming, and pointing game birds wonderfully. It was time, her heat was up; with the sound of the whistle, the hunt was on. Hazel was doing great! She located every bird in the field, but…today she felt like chasing the birds rather than pointing them. Smiling, I looked up at the sky on this terrific day in May and took a step back eleven years. That is when I had realized my love for the canine and its abilities.

Since I was ten years old my father and I religiously took our German Shorthaired Pointer, Jessie, out to hunt every weekend. At such a young age I observed the incredible natural talents that Jessie possessed. This dog never ceased to amaze me. My father and I never taught this dog anything—that is what was magical. When we brought her out to work in the fields, she just knew what had to be done. Jessie hunted the fields and forests vigorously with great desire and intensity, locating pheasants and pointing them stylishly, at times from great distances. My father would step in and flush the pheasant while Jessie remained steady through wing and shot. She retrieved the bird directly to hand. Now, many dogs have outstanding natural ability, but Jessie's was superior to most. Many dogs must be shown what they can do, and then you must manage their abilities to work together as a team.

I believe Jessie came into my life to show me what direction I should take. She taught me much about how, and to what degree, dogs use their instincts to get what they want. Once my overall attention became fixed on the canine, I began to spend a lot of time with these animals. If Jessie taught me as much as she did, then I figured others could do the same. And because I was known as a good kid in the community, providing a service that was positive, needed, and free, nobody turned me down. This enabled me to work with an array of pure and mixed breed dogs of all ages and personalities.

Throughout my youth, I concentrated primarily on basic obedience and some bird dog training. By the time I was in high school, friends and many of my teachers were impressed with my experience and abilities. While in high school I even worked with two of my teachers' dogs. Talk about student–teacher role reversal! Some teachers, as well as my family, wanted me to pursue what they perceived as more worthy career goals, because I was an excellent student. They never considered the dogs any more than a hobby.

Completely absorbed in my mission to become a successful dog trainer, I had two monumental experiences influence me. These experiences, together with the several hundred dogs I had worked with up to this point, created the canine communicator and handler that I am today. One marvelous experience was researching the habits and interactions of wolves for over a year. This was a priceless investment of time, especially after all the work I had done with dogs. It also provided me with a chance to learn the similarities and differences between the wild and domestic canine.

The second eye-opener was having the pleasure of working with an old friend of mine in the northern Catskills of upstate New York for about a year. He is a fantastic trainer overall, especially when it comes to hunting dogs. A real mountain man twice my age, he had walked a path similar to mine in his youth. We not only share many views, but birthdays as well. This man is of great character, and during that year I grew to love him like a big brother. He has shown me many things that enhanced my capabilities, and has taught me much about myself that made me an even better handler. Having lived in "my" canine world up to that point, his input allowed me to define my own style and methods of teaching our four-legged companions.

At this stage I had been studying canine nutrition for a couple years. I have continued to study it to better understand how to condition the canine athlete. I have also worked in both private and emergency veterinary hospitals for over three years, as a veterinary technician on a part-time basis. I did this mainly to support my young business and to further complete my understanding of the canine mind and body. When I was seventeen I officially opened Canine Instinct. My work with people's dogs within area communities around Glenford, New York, where I have lived all my life, continually grew. For the next four years my only advertising was word of month. To this day, most of my dogs come from previous and existing clients. I teach dogs at home and at other people's houses. I instruct one-on-one and group sessions, covering basic and advanced obedience; tracking; agility; Frisbee; waterfowl, and upland bird dog training; and occasionally seminars on canine behavior.

After having worked with over one thousand dogs in my young life, I hope that you receive a wealth of knowledge from what I am going to share with you. Enjoy!

Oh—by the way—Hazel was tested in NAVHDA that September and received a nearly perfect score across the board.

Kyle Warren and his Wirehaired Vizsla, Hazel

Canine Instinct's Education

I have had wonderful experiences with a few select humans who have enriched my knowledge, but a tremendous amount of credit goes to all of the dogs that I have worked with over the years. The following list (as of January 2006) is the main reason that I have decided to share some of my knowledge with you, so that it might help you get the most out of your canine companion and for your canine to get the most out of you, the owner! I am proud to say that I have had one-on-one relationships with these canine breeds in a training atmosphere:

1. German Shepherd: 212
2. Labrador Retriever: 141
3. Rottweiler: 101
4. Mixed Breeds: 137
5. Pit Bull: 69
6. German Shorthaired Pointer: 46
7. Siberian Husky: 46
8. Golden Retriever: 63
9. Doberman Pinscher: 45
10. Boxer: 37
11. Brittany: 27
12. Springer Spaniel: 26
13. Cocker Spaniel: 20
14. Border Collie: 13
15. Akita: 13
16. Chow Chow: 12

17. Jack Russell Terrier: 12
18. Hungarian Vizsla: 12
19. English Setter: 14
20. Great Dane: 11
21. Australian Shepherd: 11
22. Blue Heeler: 11
23. Beagle: 15
24. Norwegian Elkhound: 10
25. English Bulldog: 13
26. Standard Poodle: 9
27. Greyhound: 8
28. Rhodesian Ridgeback: 12
29. German Wirehaired Pointer: 7
30. Bullmastiff: 8
31. Yorkshire Terrier: 6
32. Alaskan Malamute: 6
33. West Highland White Terrier: 6
34. Blue Tick Coonhound: 5
35. Flat Coat Retriever: 6
36. Sheba Inu: 5
37. Irish Setter: 5
38. Chesapeake Bay Retriever: 8
39. Scottish Terrier: 4
40. Dalmatian: 4
41. Basenji: 3
42. Airedale Terrier: 6
43. Weimaraner: 7
44. Leonberger: 3

45. Bernese Mountain Dog: 3
46. Hungarian Wirehaired Vizsla: 2
47. Boston Terrier: 2
48. Fox Terrier: 2
49. Samoyed: 2
50. Shetland Sheepdog: 12
51. Wirehaired Pointing Griffon: 2
52. Saint Bernard: 2
53. Dachshund: 2
54. Pembroke Welsh Corgi: 2
55. Bouvier des Flanders: 2
56. Neapolitan Mastiff: 2
57. Miniature Pinscher: 2
58. Munsterlander: 1
59. Tervuren: 2
60. Belgium Malinois: 1
61. Bichon Frise: 2
62. Bloodhound: 1
63. Cairn Terrier: 1
64. Kuvasz: 1
65. Great Pyrenees: 2
66. Newfoundland: 6
67. Keeshond: 1
68. Gordon Setter: 1
69. Labradoodle: 6
70. Soft-Coated Wheaten Terrier: 5
71. Bull Terrier: 7
72. Toy Poodle: 3

73. Maltese: 4

74. Llewellin Setter: 5

75. Pug: 6

76. Black and Tan
    Coonhound: 1

77. Shiloh Shepherd: 1

78. Deerhound: 1

79. Wolfhound: 1

80. Afghan Hound: 1

81. French Bulldog: 2

82. Brazilian Mastiff: 1

83. Beauceron: 3

84. English Pointer: 3

85. Italian Greyhound: 1

86. Rough-Coated Collie: 3

87. Bearded Collie: 1

88. American Bulldog: 2

89. Japanese Chin: 1

Selecting A Companion

Responsibilities

Some serious thought should go into the selection of a companion dog. There are many considerations, such as space, time, and expense. An impulse buy at a pet shop "because a puppy is so cute" might turn out to be a nightmare for both dog and owner. Are you able to provide the proper environment, where the dog can have ample space to live? Do you have the time to both *care for* and *have fun with* the dog? Walking the dog three or more times a day, feeding, grooming, exercising, and socializing are all factors to take into account before getting a companion dog. Lastly, having a dog is not an inexpensive proposition. Food, routine and emergency vet bills, toys, and more are necessary costs of which to be aware. These are just some of the obligations of a responsible canine owner.

Pup or Adult

An additional decision to make is whether to choose a puppy or an adult dog. Housebreaking, immaturity, high energy, and extra attention might not be as much of a concern with some adult dogs. If the companion dog is to be a working dog, will you have the time to train a puppy up to working status?

Male or Female

Another factor to consider is gender—do you want a male or female? In my experience, whoever spends the most time with the canine is usually the person who the dog will bond to the most. However, opposites naturally attract, so male dogs tend to bond closer to female owners, and female dogs tend to bond closer to male owners. In my experience, the best working relationships are those with owners who choose a canine companion of the opposite gender. Female dogs will give female owners a more difficult time in training, and male dogs will give male owners a more difficult time as well. Now, I can provide firsthand examples where these statements have not held true, but on the whole, this is the norm.

The typical personalities of the male and female canine are very different from one another. The male usually sees life as a game and looks for stimulation more actively than the female; at times the male needs to leave his present environment to find stimulation. He is a little more carefree about his and others' behaviors. However, males can be very needy and inse-cure, always wanting to be near their owner, especially when the owner is a female.

The female dog is often a deeper thinker and takes life more seriously. She does not roam as frequently because she is preoccupied with making sure all is well on the home front. Females are usually less tolerant than males and are generally not as forgiving.

Multidog Households

There are ramifications to bringing a new dog or dogs into preexisting dog environments. I usually recom-mend that if a person has a male, to get a female as a second dog, and vice versa. As mentioned earlier regarding owners and dogs of the same gender, con-frontation can occur; this is much more likely among dogs of the same gender. This is because they are more directly in competition with each other, both for the owner's attention, as well as for their status vis-à-vis the same gendered dog within the pack. If there are two or more dogs and both genders are present, then usually I recommend that the new dog be a male—again because to a male life is more of a game and he does not take things so personally. This would therefore make it much easier to introduce another canine into an established pack. However, I love my girls and most often prefer them over the boys.

Picking a Pup

Picking a puppy is always a joy, and I am sure most of us who have ever gone to pick one out, nearly always came home with one! Selecting a puppy requires important observations. One of my personal rules of thumb to follow is "an average puppy makes a great dog." What is an average pup? It is the one that is not withdrawn from its littermates nor is it the one that is constantly pawing at your legs. It is a puppy that is with its littermates because it wants to play and to be among its pack members. This puppy is usually a great dog. Of course, there could be many in one litter, and there *should* be if the pups are of good enough bloodlines to show consistent quality. It is not impossible for a pup's personality to change completely by the time it is ten months old, but if you cultivate desired personality traits from birth, very often the only change is normal maturity.

Choosing an Adult Dog

Choosing an adult dog can be more difficult than choosing a pup. There are many variables to consider. Abuse, acquired or innate phobias, a lack of socialization, and poor development are just a few concerns. The more you know about a dog's history, the better. Many who sell or adopt out adult dogs will allow a trial period. I highly recommend that you take advantage of this opportunity. However, these trial periods are not quite adequate, generally speaking. Not enough time is allotted to give the canine adequate time to become accustomed to its new environment. When dealing with adult dog selection, you should apply the following adage: "What you see is what you get." Expose the dog to every person and every animal in its new family. Go over the daily routine and look for anything that might spark an obvious conflict. Taking these steps will help you decide whether the dog will work out or not. If the dog responds negatively to anything, then I would not consider keeping this canine because it has a greater chance of causing havoc rather than an asymptomatic dog. It is also likely to have issues in other areas unknown as yet. I would recommend that dogs displaying socialization or behavior problems be placed in single-dog households. Dogs that display problems are not incapable of being adaptable, they will just require more training, so unless you are prepared for a challenge, I would suggest you grade very conservatively.

Purebred or Mixed Breed

Selecting the proper purebred or mixed breed dog is very important. The *number two* reason why people have problems with their dogs is that they have chosen a breed that is incompatible with their household. This is only second to a lack of high-quality communication between humans and their canines. I recommend that you write out a list of your favorite breeds and your typical weekly schedule, and then go through a good breed book. It is important to write down the maintenance requirements of the dog: exercise, grooming, any special breed care—these are all important to note. Match up the weekly schedule to the dog's maintenance requirements. Using this list, you should then further investigate the breeds that best match your life style before you bring one home. You can then get a better understanding of what living with any particular breed entails. If you have the opportunity go to several breeders and meet multiple dogs of the breed to familiarize yourself with the breed more. This is probably the best way for the average person to choose a breed of dog.

A Note on Health

Of all the factors to consider when choosing a companion dog, the canine's health is the most important. Unless you are looking for a dog that is hard to place because of health problems, you usually will want a healthy dog. Take it from me—there is nothing that feels worse than having a beautiful, witty, lovable dog that has crippling hip dysplasia. All the qualities are there for it to become a wonderful family dog, show dog, and/or working dog, but it has trouble becoming any of these because of a physical defect. It can be heart breaking. When selecting a companion dog, health is vital. Look at pedigrees, meet the dog's parents, and ask for medical backgrounds. Unfortunately, all of these caveats may go out the window when you see that cute little ball of fur. Try to keep a clear head—I know it is not easy.

Summary of Key Points

🦅 Acknowledge all the necessary responsibilities that accompany dog ownership.

🦅 Have ample space in a proper environment, as well as the time to feed, groom, socialize, and exercise the dog.

🦅 Be aware of the financial obligations associated with food, with toys, and with routine and emergency vet bills.

🦅 Puppies require more time with respect to housebreaking, immaturity, and high energy.

🦅 Owners and dogs of the opposite genders tend to have a more homeostatic relationship.

🦅 Males look at life more as a game, may wander to locate stimulation, often carefree but at times insecure and clingy.

🦅 Females are deeper thinkers and take everything more seriously. They prefer to tend to the home front. Forgiveness is not always the way of a female dog, despite it being the nature of the species.

🦅 In many cases, same-gendered dogs are in direct competition with each other.

🦅 "An average pup makes a great dog." Choose the pup that appears like most of its littermates socially, not too assertive or passive. Good bloodlines should mean larger numbers of "average pups."

🦅 Check adult dogs' history in detail for physical

and emotional problems prior to adoption or purchase. It is best to apply the rule "what you see is what you get." Take the dog for a trial period to assess it in your home environment and to socialize the dog to common forms of stimulation.

🐾 A leading reason for problems with dogs is that people choose the wrong purebred or mixed breed. Go through a good breed book to look at breed profiles.

🐾 Health is a paramount concern—researching any dog's background thoroughly may save you headaches and heartaches.

Raising A Canine

Housebreaking

Housebreaking entails the control of elimination. The number one reason for success in controlling elimination with the average pup is due to handler anticipation. Let's begin with an eight-week-old pup. Key times to anticipate elimination are after the pup wakes up, even if it has only been asleep for five minutes; after eating or drinking; whenever the pup gets very stimulated, which is usually during (any time the pup disappears from where it is being stimulated—go find that pup quickly!) and after play (within fifteen to twenty minutes, maximum). Taking all of these times into consideration, keep in mind that the average eight-week-old pup will eliminate possibly five to fifteen times per day. Please make sure that the pup is receiving the proper amount of food. Food does not take long to get from one end to the other! If you feed the pup more than the necessary, the problem will be compounded. You cannot take the pup outside too much—the more the pup goes potty outside, the more it will want to go potty outside.

Up to four months of age, I recommend feeding three times per day. Over four months of age, I suggest feeding twice per day, dividing the portions equally. I fully support the following canine formulas, which are of the highest quality: Martins Formula, Fromm, Innova, and Wellness, in that order. There are other good foods available—these are just several that I know and stand behind. All four of these companies have excellent literature on their products.

When the pup goes out to go potty, give praise and say "potty" every time he or she empties bowels or bladder. If you do this, your pup will eventually go potty on command all the time. A handler certainly has enough times to practice this command. Having said "potty" each time my pups went, I now can pull off the highway, say the word, and be back on the road in under a minute—just like a pit stop in NASCAR.

Using the Crate

I do use a crate to aid in potty training and house manners. I recommend purchasing a crate that the pup will fit into when fully grown. There should only be enough room in the crate for the pup to stand up and lie down in. Block off any extra area with a solid object until the pup grows big enough to need that space. Purchase an enclosed kennel, like the Vari-Kennel. Enclosed crates are recommended over the complete wire crates, mainly because the crate should be a place of security. The wire crates leave the pup exposed and feeling vulnerable. Place the crate in the room where the dog will be sleeping on a permanent basis. I only place the pup in the crate when nobody will be home. If the owner wants to teach the dog to sleep in the crate at night, that is acceptable. *The crate is only used in a positive sense*, never as a form of punishment.

The crate is used to teach the pup to sleep while the family is away. It is also used to teach the pup to control elimination, and to be nondestructive. I usually start to trust the pup in small doses outside the crate at six months of age, or until the pup has rectified all of its problems that can be solved with crate training. Yes, there are some dogs that can never be trusted, but most can be trusted in time. *Food and water should never be in the crate.* This encourages elimination and a real big mess! Toys and a sturdy, safe, absorbent blanket should be in the crate at all times. Toys that I recommend placing in the crate are ropes, any Kong products, and real sterilized bones. The bones should be thick ones that commonly do not splinter. Do make sure that the condition of the rope is good and not frayed. Other toys or treats that I support are Greenies, Booda Bones, braided rawhides, and real meat bones. These items I recommend under supervision because a piece could break off, causing the pup difficulty. The pup should have access to water at all times other than when it is in the crate. Sometimes having a radio or television on at low volume (or even a fan on) helps relax the pup and muffle any noises it might hear that could be upsetting. The pup should be weaned from the crate gradually, roughly over a month's time. If the pup regresses due to undesirable behavior, then for several days place it back in the crate when unsupervised before attempting to trust the pup again. While someone is home, the crate door should be left open so that the dog can go in and out as it pleases. Often the dog will view the crate as a den. When the home environment gets hectic, the dog can often be found in its crate. The crate should be available to the dog throughout its entire life.

Exercise

Exercise is very important for every canine to have from puppyhood through adulthood. Do some research on your dog's breed to see how much exercise is recommended. A lack of physical exercise can lead to a lack of mental exercise as well. If there is only one dog in your household, then see if there are dogs in the neighborhood to set up play dates. When the workday is done, go out in the backyard and play fetch for a half hour. Take the dog for at least a ten-minute walk a few times a day. Do a formal obedience session with the dog for ten to twenty minutes. Try to make some or all of these activities part of the dog's daily routine.

Socialization and Desensitization

Socialization and desensitization are also important in dog training. My approach is determined by the age of the dog. I will teach a mature dog that has never been socialized some basic obedience as well as respect for the handler prior to exposing this unruly dog to distractions that very well could induce undesired behaviors. For a puppy two to four months old, on the other hand, I make sure that while being socialized only the "no" command is applied, when needed, to reinforce concepts of manners. To properly socialize the pup, the stimuli should be introduced gradually, in accord with how well the pup is adapting.

To ensure a positive experience with a stimulus, the handler must introduce only controlled stimuli in a controlled environment. The handler must know what the behavior and/or actions will or will not be in relation to interacting with the canine. No variables can be in the environment; this could cause the dog to have a negative experience with a stimulus. It should be exposed to people of all shapes, sizes, ages, personalities, professions, and as many ethnicities as possible. Exposure to various people in an array of professions is extremely valuable—desk workers, butchers, and everything else in between! A person's occupation tells the canine what the person does and where. A person might upset a canine depending on how he or she smells! Again, the handler needs to be selective with the people who will be used, because strictly positive interaction between humans and the canine, using controlled variables, is being emphasized.

Canines should be exposed to other canines outside the family. Noises of any kind also require the handler's attention. It is wise to expose the canine to other animals that it might come across in its life. Having the dog see as many objects as possible helps as well. As the socialization and desensitization proceeds, the handler can observe and take note of any fears or dislikes that the canine exhibits toward anything it is introduced to. This process helps identify problems that the handler must attend to ensure that these issues do not become dangerous situations. Canines on a whole do not like change, so it is important to expose them to as many variables of the human world as possible to discover what might trigger undesirable behaviors in the individual canine so that any undesirable behaviors can be eliminated.

It is imperative that socialization occurs not only at eight weeks of age, but throughout a dog's development. My personal opinion is that the dog should be aggressively socialized and desensitized up until the age of two. At this point, I believe the canine's mind is fairly solidified with preferred concepts of socialization and desensitization. If an eight-week-old pup is exposed to a stimulus and displays a desired reaction, it does not necessarily mean that two years later it will respond in the same fashion. Ideally, the canine should be consistently and routinely exposed to stimuli up until the age of two. After the dog reaches the age of two, periodic exposure of the dog to these stimuli should suffice. I do believe that up until two years of age it is necessary to aggressively socialize the dog so that the handler knows the likely reactions of the canine. Socialization and desensitization helps to ensure safety and long-lasting desired behaviors.

To ensure leaving a positive impression with your pup,

I recommend that obedience not be used during socialization and desensitization before four months of age. The puppy is usually in a euphoric state of mind, and any reinforcement of something the puppy does not want to do while interacting with another animal or person could be construed as a negative experience. When "negative" moments occur, separate the canine from the stimulus. In the future avoid this particular stimulus until some obedience has been done with the canine. Once the canine has respect for you as the handler and an education to fall back on, then you can return to the dog's problem area(s).

From the time you get a pup, the giving and taking of toys should be done at random on a regular basis to help prevent and/or identify any aggressive possession issues. The same goes for food. Stroking the pup while placing a hand in the food bowl will help it associate eating as a team effort as opposed to a greedy, selfish moment. Toys and food are very common problem areas within the household. It is worth taking the time to make sure the pup acts safely and respectfully toward its handler and its peers.

Summary of Key Points

✎ *The number one key to housebreaking is anticipation.*

✎ *An eight-week-old pup will eliminate as much as fifteen times or more per day. You cannot take a puppy outside too much.*

❧ Feed appropriate quantities; it does not take long for food to go from one end to the other end. Feed a pup three times per day up to four months of age, then twice a day after four months old.

❧ Say "potty" or another word of your choice any time the pup eliminates to teach it to eliminate on command in the future.

❧ The crate is used to teach a dog to sleep and not be destructive while the owner is away. The dog should only be placed in the crate when nobody is home and at night, if preferred. Purchase a crate for the pup that it will fit in once grown.

❧ Enclosed crates are best.

❧ Place crate in a quiet, comfortable room.

❧ No food or water in the crate. Only nonedible toys in the crate.

❧ After about four months of crate training, you can start to gradually wean the pup out of the crate while away from home. If the dog is bad then place back in crate.

❧ Exercise is very important mentally and physically. A lack of exercise can result in an increase of bad behavior. Multiple walks and/or obedience sessions each day can emotionally center a dog.

❧ In dog training, socialization and desensitization are interchangeable.

❧ A pup two to four months old should receive abundant attention and love, in addition to manner encouragement.

✎ A pup should be exposed to new experiences in a very controlled environment to ensure a positive experience.

✎ A person's occupation can tell a dog a great deal about the person (their smell). The socializing and desensitizing process allows an owner to see any discomforts that the dog might have.

✎ Dogs do not like change. Dogs should be aggressively socialized and desensitized up to two years of age.

My Approach With The Canine

A Canine's Rank

There are two aspects to a canine's rank. One is the natural rank that is determined by the dog's personality; the other is a rank determined by the other dogs within the pack. There are naturally dominant, carefree, and submissive personalities, with variations within each of these three descriptions. For illustration, I can explain canine rank using a pack of ten canines. In nature, packs vary in size from two up to twelve canines, and some packs can even be larger. I use a total of ten because that is the average number of dogs in a pack. The same principles apply regardless of the size of the pack. Number one is the alpha dog, at the top of the social ladder. Number ten is the most submissive dog, at the bottom of the social ladder.

I can label two dogs in the same pack as naturally ranking number three dogs. When in a pack, one of the canines will rise to a number two or sink to a number four depending upon the other pack members. Often, a dog's natural status is different from its social status in its' family unit. Providing the canine is not of higher status on the social ladder than the owner (once trained), the handler must allow the dogs to determine their social status among themselves. The handler only intervenes if the dogs are looking to cause injury to each other in order to establish rank.

As the handler, you are primarily concerned with the canine's natural rank. This is because you are working with the dog one on one, and you are presenting yourself with quality communication and guidance that should gain you the respect as an alpha dog. Of the over thirteen hundred dogs I have worked with, I have experienced less than ten *true* alpha dogs. These are dogs that *refuse* to step down from the throne, despite an ideal presentation, which is how a handler communicates with a dog on the highest level emotionally and physically. These *true* alphas will often defend their destiny *at all costs*! Often I have heard people say that their dog is an alpha dog. Statistically, I am ninety-nine percent sure that they are wrong. Poor communication and a lack of effort are two of the main reasons for these false conclusions. I have known some dogs to be labeled alpha dogs that are actually as low as number eight in rank. The dogs simply know the owner's ins and outs better than the owner knows himself or herself.

Here is how I label personality traits with natural and social ranks. The alpha dog is the number one dog in the pack. He will step down for no one. He will be ousted from the pack before stepping down. This canine was blueprinted to be at the top. However, this does not mean that this dog will not listen at all; however, it does indicate that in any environment where stimulated by something or someone other than the handler, the canine will never hesitate to go to the stimulus. A dog's respect for the handler is challenged in a distractive environment of any kind, but this is not the only issue with an alpha because this dog feels he is at the top of the heap. These dogs are very stressful to live with, and depending upon the household, they sometimes have to be removed because alpha dogs will defend their status regardless of consequence. Alpha dogs are usually cocky, confident, and like to throw their weight around, especially when feeling inferior. They are generally not good with other dogs in a human world because they are *exceptionally* controlling—the other dog never catches a break from the alpha dog, who is often a tyrant. I have only dealt with a handful of dogs that I would place within this rank, and only one of them was a female; the rest were males. Common sense dictates it would be wise to avoid these dogs.

The number two dog in the pack is my personal favorite in the pack. In my experience, these canines tend to be females. This canine is very interesting. She has some of the same traits as the alpha dog, but has much more to offer the handler. She is bold, confident, serious, but playful. Usually she adores a good handler. Out of the entire pack, I sense this dog is the most creative thinker. She has the ability to think outside the box and most canines do not do that on their own.

Very often these dogs are high energy and always on the go. They are true workaholics. They are always on duty. This canine is the ultimate working companion. She has drive, desire, and team spirit; she will remain at the top of her game for more years than most dogs do. Despite the high praise I give this dog, she is not for everyone. The combination of all the qualities inherent in this dog can work against a handler if he does not use it to his advantage. At times, this ultimate working dog makes its own decisions about how to get the job done, and sometimes the handler disagrees, but being the dominant dog that she is, she assertively sticks to her game plan to complete the task. A good handler will work the dog in a fashion and in an environment that keeps the dog connected, until the handler needs the canine to pull some tricks out of her sleeve in specific situations. Unfortunately, these alpha dogs frequently live a restricted life because people let their talents turn into terrors, mostly due to ignorance. This canine has great potential.

Canines ranking from numbers three to five within a pack are so similar that often the only way to really decide their rank is to take their interaction with other dogs into consideration. I believe that these three ranks make up the largest group of canines in the canine population. The number three dogs can get fairly dominant on occasion, but other than that, the canines within these three ranks are nearly equals. Characteristics that I often associate with these canines are as follows: a carefree personality in terms of activities and environments, the potential to be slavishly obedient for a good handler, a "by the book" kind of dog, a follower, an affectionate companion, and when others push them around, they push back. Possessiveness can be an issue from time to time with these dogs, but many problems usually can be worked out easily with a bit of work. I would, on a whole, recommend these dogs for the average family. In general, they are naturally good-natured; if any aggression is displayed, others usually induce it. For a novice handler, this dog is a good choice.

The number six dog is a transitional pack member. I do not want to classify this canine along with dogs ranking three to five, because it can display signs of a naturally submissive personality. However, I do not want to place it with canines ranking seven to nine, because this dog does not show outward signs of insecurity without provocation. Unlike its surrounding pack members, this canine is almost incapable of aggression. I have never worked with a number six dog that had any aggressive faults. I say "almost never" because there is never a guarantee. Number six dogs are good dogs to own but greatly limited in numbers.

I place canines ranking as numbers seven to nine collectively in a separate group. On a whole, they are very similar, but number seven certainly is not as naturally submissive as the other two ranks. These dogs display traits of insecurity, submissiveness toward pack members, and a closed-minded attitude; without the help of the handler, they are incapable of creative thinking outside the box and often they have difficulty having fun because they are usually dwelling on bad things, such as other pack members hurting them and feeling sorry for themselves. To decide who is what among these three ranks, pack interaction is almost a must. Dogs ranked seven to nine do not make good working dogs under normal circumstances. They can make acceptable family dogs, but they should never be trusted, especially with children, due to possible aggression.

The number ten canine in the pack is a mess! Boy...oh boy...does this dog have problems! This canine shares some traits with the canines that rank from seven to nine in the pack. However, this dog's problems intensify twofold. In the past there have been two dogs for which I have recommended medication for that ranked as number ten dogs in the pack. Everyone always feels sorry for this dog, but as a family pet stay away from it! Naturally, there are only a few number ten dogs; most are ranked as such due to social influence.

My pack of ten system has worked well in helping me explain to my clients where their dogs are "coming from." If you plug your canine into my system, it might tell you a lot about your instinctive four-legged friend.

Communicating with the Canine

When discussing the roots of the domestic canine, people often misinterpret and misapply concepts of the wild canine to the domestic canine. In my experience, I have learned to clearly distinguish what I perceive to be the similarities and differences. The most common mistake by owners, in my opinion, is the correction that involves grabbing the scruff of the neck. It is an absolutely natural correction in the wild. But most handlers reading this book are not in the wild, and the handler is not a dog. Dogs are simple creatures, but they are not dumb. They realize the individual correcting them is not a dog, and thus this is not a natural correction. Canines most definitely get the message that the handler disapproves of their actions, but only because they can reason, not because the handler understands the dog's instinctive mind. So yes, I am saying not to grab the dog by the scruff of the neck for a correction! The only time I grab my dogs' scruff is when they are *little* pups, to pick them up and while playing—both are positive usages.

The main similarity between a wolf and a dog is in their thought processes, particularly in the way in which they learn and analyze life within their environment. The wolf naturally learns about its environment and analyzes through observation all on its own. The domestic dog usually has difficulty doing this because it is not in a natural environment. Companion dogs live in the world of humans, not the world of wolves. Their brains function like a wolf's: it is a highly instinctive brain, with a blueprint that they are born to follow. It is based on nature: earth, trees, grass, wildlife, and so on. Canines do not naturally understand being tied up, TVs, four walls, vehicles, traffic cones, or Spiderman action figures. There is nothing instinctive about these objects to a canine, and because their reasoning is based on their instincts, they can have a difficult time adjusting to human norms.

Canines think very methodically—one thing at a time.

They can think quickly—however, one thing at a time. The last thing you tell a dog is the last thing it remembers. Whether or not the dog listens depends upon whether it understands what you as handler are saying and whether it respects you as handler (or not). Dogs can have an amazing memory. Remember, the last command given is what is on its mind. If you say "sit—down—stay," then "stay" is what the dog has on its mind. This can also be applied to the "quality" of a training session. If the dog has been worked for fifteen minutes and you have kept the energy positive and flowing nicely, the canine can remain in a good frame of mind, thus allowing the session to end on a positive note. The longer the session, the more difficult it is to keep the energy upbeat and positive, especially basic obedience. You could work with a dog for five hours, and if the last five minutes has a negative tone, then the dog more than likely views the activity as negative. The dog still retains parts of the session, but it is not viewed as positive due to ending on a bad note. I recommend short but frequent sessions—anywhere from five- to twenty-minute sessions, two to four times a day, until the dog is doing satisfactory work for the handler. This is for basic obedience. Like everything else in life, the more you do something, the better you get at what you are doing. Handlers need to feel out their dogs to know where the dogs' boiling points are, so they know when to call it quits. The handler should always end the session when the handler wants to; however, the handler should make sure the dog is aware that the handler is the one terminating the session—not the dog.

The canine has blueprints in its head that it bases both its own functions on as well as the functions of others. To understand the transfer issue, which is the dog listening better to the teacher than the owner, I need to explain the elements of love, respect, and trust to help you understand the role each plays in your relationship with your dog. The owner's relationship is based on love, and his or her history with the dog is *usually* an unruly one, or at least not one of obedience on the canine's part. The owner has established security and comfort, but also a lack of control, simply because the owner has never shown the dog otherwise. Even the most mild, easygoing dog needs to know *why* it must listen to the owner.

Recall that the alpha dog is number one in a pack of ten canines. A dog is given the role of alpha whether it wants it or not due to a lack of communication on the owner's behalf. The owner hopes to gain respect through proper presentation with practice. I, the teacher, on the other hand, have come into the relationship with a clean slate. With me, the dog has never gotten away with anything. I establish control from the start with black and white guidance that the dog understands completely. The dog usually realizes, because of my ideal presentation, that I have known how to do this for a long time ago. My most dominant dogs are willing, in general, to step down from the throne for me. That is not the problem here. It is taking someone below the dog on the social ladder, and placing that person, the owner, above his or her dog, when it has always been the reverse. My role is completely understood, and most of the time accepted by the dog. The owner's previous role was understood and appreciated, but now the dog sees this change in status and says to itself, "Whoa-whoa-whoa, wait a minute here! The alpha, the teacher, is now taking my owner, who is below me on the social ladder, and placing my owner above me?!" There is nothing in the canine blueprint saying it has to listen to more than one alpha per environment. A *multi-alpha* environment is a foreign concept to a dog. Unfortunately, as the dog is living in the human world, this belief must be ousted, so both you and I, the handlers, can function as alphas while teaching the canine.

Honestly, at best, I would say that there is only a forty to fifty percent transfer from myself to the owner. It takes several months of consistent hard work to reinforce my standards. That way, the owner becomes as identical to me as possible and thus achieves maximum performance from the dog. Good handling is valuable to the owner. A novice handler must concentrate on what he or she is doing more so than about what the dog is doing! *The dog can never handle better than the handler.* In the first few weeks, there can be a lot of friction between the owner and the dog, until the owner's handling improves to the point to where the canine responds promptly to the owner's good guidance. If only up to fifty percent or less of what I do transfers to the owner, then it is my responsibility to teach both the owner and the dog what is required to function together as a team.

Most of my canine clients thoroughly enjoy the

communication despite the material being taught. Many of the dogs that I see every week cannot wait to see me, even though I bust their chops about their problem areas. They would love for me to spend the entire day just interacting with them because the communication that we share is far more connected than what they have with any other human. If through quality communication I can keep the canine focused on the tasks that I am demanding, and I remain in communication with the canine, encouraging a positive frame of mind, then the canine is almost forced to be positive toward our work. Since the dog thinks very methodically, one thing at a time, fluent handling essentially does not allow the canine to think about anything other than what I want it to think about.

Dogs are very grey creatures, in that they read in between the lines, so that as stated earlier we must deliver our messages in black and white to make our presentation clean, cut, and dry. To reach the level of success that I mark as a goal, we must only tell a canine a command once, and then fix it the second time. Make sure you are following this rule: *First time told, second time fixed.* This simply means that if the dog does not do what it is told the first time, then make it do it the second time. If the handler tells the dog to sit, and the dog does not sit, then wait one second and make the dog sit. The canine must learn that there are no options with the handler—if there are then I guarantee that the canine will choose everything but the handler's desired response.

As a handler, you want to have as little negative

interaction as possible, both verbally and physically. I touch the dog in a negative sense as little as possible. You should use the leash as much as possible to correct the dog. If the dog gets up from a stay, do not push it forcefully back into a stay. Walk the dog quickly and nicely back to the stay spot, and repeat the command. The leash is the handler's main tool until respect is gained. I call the leash a "freedom stick." When in hand, the dog knows the handler has control; when out of hand, the dog "flips the handler the paw," as I say. A leash and collar is all that is needed for my teaching. We never use prong collars or shock collars. In the basic obedience chapter there is a brief section on training devices and their benefits that you can use, if needed. If used properly, my methods will educate you to gain maximum cooperation from your canine.

What is nice about dogs is that whatever the handler puts into them, the handler gets out of them. The bad thing about dogs is that seldom will they do more than what you make them do. Make sure to never give a correction without a command. Do not *ever* give a dog a correction for something and not let it know what it did wrong. Only give a command initially when you want the canine to do something and repeat it only if the dog makes a mistake. Do not constantly repeat the command if the dog is doing the task properly, because the canine might think that it made a mistake and/or does not understand you. If you make this error, you could very well *encourage* the dog to make mistakes. Please, only give a command if it will be followed through—if not, it only emphasizes to the canine a lack of control.

Teaching a canine properly takes tim[...]
Rome wasn't built in a day—they worked[...]
tently everyday. And do not use treats! Giv[...]
a form of bribery and only works optimally in[...]
mally distractive environment, where there [...]
reason for a priority shift in the dog. It enterta[...]
fellow humans and makes the canine happy, but the
handler is never happy when it is crunch time. The
treat is the priority, and there will always be something
more important than a treat. At its best performance,
the canine will still not make the handler its number
one priority. In many cases, treats are used in place of
communication skills.

Certainly heavy-handed techniques are outdated,
frowned upon, and inferior to other methods.
Depending on how violent the handler becomes with
the canine, the dog will either retreat to total submis-
sion, or become defensive or offensive, both of which
often results in aggressive behavior. Again, I attribute
this method to a poor handler profile, including a lack
of communication abilities. Love, respect, and trust,
which are central to my method, are extremely valuable commodities to a dog once the handler has earned
them. Along with being understood by their peers,
dogs thoroughly enjoy verbal and physical praise from
humans. Canines are extremely intelligent in comparison to most other animals, but if you *truly* understand
them, you will learn how uncomplicated they really
are. A handler's natural ability certainly affects
the results obtained. My methods are simple,

equally important,

. There is a tremen-

ine, but it all comes

andler to learn are

is or her dog, and

me say this, but the

do with your dog is

is necessary to achieve

wever, it by no means is

.....ng. because working a dog takes

..p a very small percentage of its day, it is when the dog evaluates the owner the least. Even if the owner is a real die hard and works the dog a half-hour every day, there is still twenty-three and a half hours out of the day left for the dog to consider how the owner is doing as a handler. Great handling is surely one of the keys to success, but when the dog is on a take-a-break and feeling in control of itself due to a lack of direct attention and not being given commands from the handler, then that is the time the dog is doing most of its evaluating of the owner. A handler needs to establish a baseline presentation to the dog. If, for instance, at one time in the day a handler's physical movements are really fast and voice is high, and later in the day the handler's movements are slow and voice low, he or she has no baseline, no consistency. The dog will therefore not want to comply with any of the handler's commands because he or she has shown no alpha-like qualities—one of which is consistency in presentation.

A handler's attitude can greatly affect a dog's progress.

I can teach an owner technique and the understanding of the canine; however, having the right attitude often just depends on the individual. When people see my handling they say, "Wow! I don't have that much energy!" My passion for teaching the canine certainly is projected; I also have confidence and an ideal presentation. It is important to want to work with the canine.

You need discipline to work every day with your unruly student. As a novice handler, you need the confidence that you can accomplish work with the dog. I define *confidence* as being positive, upbeat, fluent, and knowing what you want from the dog. You have to let the dog know that it must impress you. When I handle a canine I always ask myself, "When I tell the dog to do this [any particular task], what are all the possible outcomes?" I identify all possible mistakes, then assume that the dog is going to make them. By thinking this way, I am fully prepared to correct any mistake that the dog might make. You must present yourself consistently regardless of the dog's presentation, which is what an alpha does.

It is very natural for the handler's performance to deteriorate as the canine's performance worsens, but this cannot happen if you are to earn respect from your dog. The handler must always remain cool, calm, collected, and focused on his or her handling. The presentation of the handler to the dog is the make or break factor. As alluded to earlier, the dog can only handle as well as the handler handles himself or herself. In fact, it is imperative that the novice handler concentrate on improving his or her handling. The sooner the handler improves, the sooner the dog improves.

The rules must be clearly defined, so that the guidance given is totally understood. Think of teaching a dog like dancing: you as handler are the lead dancer and the dog must follow the handler's lead. Feel like you are on a mission, you are going to succeed, and you are going to have fun! I have found that the more precise structure I am able to give the owner, the better the owner does as a handler and the better the dog does for its owner. There are several simple things to keep in mind when handling a dog to make sure that you always have structure so you do not deteriorate with the dog's performance. As a handler, bring the dog to you and never let the dog's actions alter your original plan. For instance, when you are heeling with the dog, draw patterns with your feet. Keep it simple with squares, triangles, circles, straight lines, "s-shaped," and "i-shaped" patterns. When walking these shapes and letters, you have a defined plan and when the canine makes a mistake you can stick to the plan. You can create your walking plans before you ever go outside with the canine. Most people just go outside to "work" with their dog and the only thing they know is that they will cover all the positive concept commands. If the handler is a person having difficulty controlling the dog when the dog starts to shut down on him or her, then these shapes and letters are great! They are especially helpful to children who are handling.

Each pattern serves a purpose. The square practices ninety-degree turns. The triangle practices forty-five degree turns. The circle practices a constant gradual turn. The straight-line practices one hundred-eighty degree turns. The "s-shaped" pattern practices tight inside and outside turns. Lastly, the "i-shaped" pattern practices frequent stops, by walking about five feet or so, then stopping, followed by one giant step and a stop (then another five feet or so, then stopping followed by one giant step and stop...). Feel free to experiment with other shapes and letters. Do remember to keep it simple. These are just some of my all time favorites. I also encourage troubled handlers, while walking with the dog, to not look at the dog much, so they do not dwell on what the dog is doing, but rather concentrate on what they themselves are doing. This concept is stated again in the Heel section.

Helping a handler learn and keep structure when working with a dog can be challenging. I have found that one of the most useful ways of improving the consistency of a handler's presentation is to practice with an invisible dog. The reason why the invisible dog is so helpful is because of what I said in the first sentence of this section about interaction effecting presentations. Since the invisible dog will listen perfectly to a handler, the handler is able to completely concentrate on what he or she is suppose to do rather than what the dog is doing. The more a handler practices with the invisible dog, the more naturally coordinated a handler will become. When a handler wants to practice correcting a mistake, then the handler simply assumes that the invisible dog made a mistake and corrects him accordingly.

Many of the first several hundred dogs that I taught were easygoing (on the whole). This allowed me to focus on a constant uniform physical presentation. A real dog that a handler is working with will most often not give a flawless presentation; therefore, the handler's presentation worsens. This is why practicing by yourself with the invisible dog is so valuable. Remember to work by yourself as the Checklist in future sections is learned. This will help you develop yourself as the focal point rather than the dog. Much of teaching a dog is being in control of yourself and having self-discipline prior to being able to discipline the dog. Many people feel uncomfortable and silly working alone. All they need is some self-confidence. Dog handling in many ways is a physical skill and can be learned. When I was young, I would practice my movements every night before going to bed. If I told people I did this for martial arts, they would think that it was entirely normal. Dog handling is no different.

One way to keep track of your progress is to keep a journal of the experiences you have training your dog. This is what I have done over the years, especially since my teachings are based on personal observations. Simply write what you see your dog doing at any time. Write as much as you are willing to do. Being a keen observer and keeping track of your experiences makes you a great handler and owner.

Love, Respect, and Trust

Love, respect, and trust are the three most important elements in any relationship, regardless of species. These three elements are the fundamental components with which you will be training your dog.

Love is the most valuable. It creates happiness, safety, comfort, and security within a relationship. Unfortunately, love has very little to do with a canine being responsive to a handler.

Respect, on the other hand, is the key element within a canine-human relationship that makes it a working relationship. I do not want you to associate the word *respect* with "fear" and "constant discipline"—that is not what I am talking about. When I allude to respect, it is in appreciation toward communication between the handler and the dog because of the handler's quality guidance. The handler is certainly viewed as having status and therefore a dominant figure; the canine, however, also thinks of the handler as a true friend. That is what separates the ideal handler and the straight-up disciplinarian. You have to earn a canine's respect. To prove yourself to a dog can be very difficult. I find that people tend to treat dogs like people, or attempt to use various training methods that a dog does not understand. If the handler cannot prove to the canine that he or she can give the canine the proper guidance necessary to do what the handler is requesting, then the dog will follow its own lead!

Communicating with a canine can be very challenging. I do feel that I have innate abilities to communicate with canines to the degree that I have had to communicate with them over the years. I cannot teach you all of my talents; however, using them, I can guide you successfully down the road to having a happy, respectful, and obedient companion. When you understand dogs, you can see what simple creatures they really are. I have both seen and made canines do amazing things. This is not because they think like we do; conversely, they use their incredible instinctive senses to reason and solve situations. We as the handlers must use these senses while working with the dog. If we do not, then these senses will surely be used against us. To make progress, you must understand the dog's "language." The two species in this relationship do not speak the same language—I am the translator. I feel very confident in stating that *all* problems that people have with their dog, ranging from the dog not listening to the basic commands to the most aggressive situations, that are acquired behaviors, stem from a lack of respect for the handler and from a lack of education. Through proper natural communication with the canine, the handler will gain respect from the dog. If there is someone to whom a canine looks to for guidance and authority, that dog will make much wiser decisions around the clock.

Dogs are what I call a *total package creature*. This means that to gain their respect, your handling has to be as flawless as possible with all the commands all the time. Once you start demanding work from a dog, it will constantly be looking for flaws, especially if it has a history of disobeying you. A prime time that you need to be on your toes is when you first try assuming control of the canine and when distractions occur; both these situations can occur at the same time. You will never have control of the canine if not when these instances arise. This is a peak time to gain mega respect from the canine if you perform well. The dog will look for excuses not to listen if you have not yet received respect from them. The more respect you gain, the less the dog will test you.

With dogs, it is the little things that count. Again, they are looking for excuses, so do the best to not let them find any! Many canines find their excuses for not listening inside the home. This is because people naturally relax and let their guard down inside the home. When the handler works outside and the dog is placed on a sit-stay from ten feet away with no leash on, the handler remains very aware of the dog's attitude and environment. In contrast, placing the dog on a sit-stay on the living room rug, five feet away, the handler may tend to become complacent. Outside, the handler remains alert due to the greater chance of harm to the dog, whereas inside, when the dog breaks the sit-stay, the handler might allow it owing to a long workday—he or she just wants to unwind and knows the dog is safe. This may not seem like a big deal. But this is when the dog takes its cheat sheet out and places the handler in the "They Cannot Control Me" category. Make sure that if a command is given that it is followed through from start to finish. If you are not in the mood or lack the energy to follow through with a command, you will give the dog a message that signifies a lack of control.

If you are viewed by the canine as simply the boss, it might be a working relationship, but not a happy one. You have to approach the dog as a friend who is trying to help the dog successfully complete a task. The rules that the handler creates along the way should be viewed as such by the dog, however, thought more of as guidance than as rules. This strictly depends on how well you can communicate with the canine. Canines *like* to do things well. The ideal handler can keep the canine's mind on task. This is accomplished through quality handling. If, while remaining positive, you can keep the canine thinking about what you want it to, then the canine is more likely to remain positive as well. Using my methods, you will maximize this needed connection. To achieve a more personal relationship with the canine, you must respect the canine as much as you expect respect from the canine. This must be a mutually respectful relationship for it to be ideal.

When working with love and respect, you really have to take the canine's individualism into account. You must walk a fine line between love and respect. If you are too compassionate, the canine will run all over you, and if you are too firm, the canine will either shut down or turn on the handler. This, generally, is how to look at it, but each canine personality will sway slightly one way or the other, usually causing you to teach the canine according to its personality.

Trust is the last component used in making my methods work. Trust is the progressive element of the relationship. You will not gain progress unless you trust your dog. Dogs learn best through trial and error. It is minimizing the error that gives the dog the understanding of the guidance and the importance of the task. You have to allow the dog to initiate a mistake before giving a correction. That is all that needs to happen. You should not allow the dog to complete a mistake—the sooner the correction the better. The canine must feel controlled but not because of you limiting the dog's actions in a physical manner. You are limiting these actions *in a psychological manner*, by not allowing the dog time to think of a plan. The canine should always view the environment in relation to the handler, as one of trust. The dog needs to learn to trust the handler in any setting. This is achieved by allowing the dog to do as it pleases and the handler explaining to the canine what are the desired and undesired actions that the canine performs throughout any given day whether it is working or involved in its own activity. I find the trust factor to be the most difficult component in the canine and handler relationship.

A Canine's Abilities

Now that you have read the previous section, take the following into consideration: The abilities that canines possess are *truly* the reasons for my devotion to this magnificent species. I work with these abilities everyday and they never cease to amaze me. In my experience, a canine's sense of smell is its most powerful tool, followed by its hearing, then its sight. The canine's sense of smell has been used for an array of tasks for centuries. A canine's world is sensed through its nose. I have heard of studies done on the canine's nose, which demonstrate its ability to smell odors over one hundred times greater than a human can detect. And, it is said that dogs can smell tracks that are up to six weeks old. That is amazing! The canine's sense of hearing has been debated as well. I have read various articles indicating that it is twice as keen as a human's ability to hear. Canines also can detect motion and see better at night than humans can. Some studies show that canines can acknowledge movement from a half-mile away. Another amazing feature of the canine that is useful is its ability to apply tremendous amounts of pressure when it bites.

The overall athletic ability of this species is absolutely amazing. All over the world today canines are used for nearly every possible occupation. Canines are used for police work, search and rescue, hunting, herding, tracking, protection, agility, locating poisonous gases and rotted telephone poles, and many other tasks. As far as I am concerned, the canine's stamina, endurance, and ability to do endless tasks rival any other mammal. You will come to agree with the figures that I have given you after you have read the later chapter containing just a few anecdotes of mine that I have included.

Most canines can learn different kinds of jobs, especially those bred for them. However, there are dogs that have more natural ability and desire than others, and those are the canines that are targeted for specific occupations. Whatever you decide to do, realize that activities are supposed to be fun. Some dogs do not want to participate. It is usually not worth the effort to try to make these dogs work. If they do not want to do whatever you are doing, try something different. Every dog is not a working dog, regardless of his or her breed. Before, or in conjunction with any occupational teaching, basic obedience is a must! You must be able to control the dog in the backyard and in social environments prior to working with what the dog was born to do.

Regardless of the task at hand, each canine *can* take different lengths of time to learn how to do its job well. Some jobs take a few months to perfect, while others take a few years. In any case, make sure the dog is doing each stage consistently well before moving on to the following stages. If the pup has difficulty or expresses disobedience in the next stage, then take a step back to the previous stage. Remember that dogs do not have deadlines. It is all about time, patience, and repetition using the right teaching methods that will give rise to long-term success.

Timetable

All of the basic obedience commands can be introduced at the same time and all can be practiced during each session. As time goes on, a handler can concentrate more on troublesome commands. It is important to practice these commands, ten to thirty minutes daily, until the dog is performing to the handler's standards. Realistically, two to six months is a normal time frame for a dog and his or her owner to accomplish the desired goals with these commands. Each dog, handler, and environment is different; therefore, each will take a different length of time to achieve success. Be patient! Remember: *No Deadlines!* You and your dog are learning together, and your dog might not want to listen to you before you prove yourself to him or her.

I normally start teaching my pups no younger than four months of age. I really enjoy teaching in the four- to eleven-month-old age bracket. Remember that puppies cannot be pushed as fast as adult dogs. I have taught dogs of all ages—the only one that said that you could not teach an old dog new tricks was the old dog! A dog is *never too old to learn*, but it certainly does get more difficult, and success occasionally does decrease as the dog ages. The length of a dog's training program is directly related to the amount of quality time put in by the handler. You can work a dog too much. I would not work a dog for more than an hour per day when it comes to basic obedience. Never practice longer than half-hour segments; I would prefer you to work in short but frequent sessions. Dogs progress much faster in three twenty-minute sessions per day, rather than one hour-long session per day. The more you do something, the better you get at it!

Playing Rough

A large percentage of the time that I spend with a dog is spent playing. As with many of my views, this one tends to be unorthodox. Playing rough is fine—no, actually, it is great! Dogs play rough, that is a fact. Dogs have a social system of respect, but no matter where a dog is on the social ladder they all play rough together. When the dogs of authority in the pack need the others' attention, they get it. Why? Because leaders tell the pack members what is acceptable and what is not. If a dog gets out of hand, then I let him or her know it by ending the play, usually with a stay. I play as rough as the dogs want, as long as it does not turn into an uncontrollable frenzy. I always discourage jumping with the no command. Actually, this is a great time to practice it because this play puts the dog in the frame of mind where he or she is likely to jump up. I love to roll around on the ground and basically *act like a dog*. Many say that you should not encourage rough play-like behavior and get down on the ground as an equal, boy…oh boy… this sounds like someone who needs to keep the animal subdued at all times, because he or she cannot communicate with the canine on a level of mutual understanding. Perhaps, this is one of the many reasons the vast majority of my canines are thrilled to see me *and listen*. They view me as a friend with alpha status that is here to have a good time. This play is good bonding time and is another way to establish a positive relationship with the dog, the way the dog wants. Just avoid the wild-eyed frenzy mode.

Tough Weather Training

During the winter as well as the summer months temperatures can be brutal. The bad stories that you hear about usually take place in the summer months while training. When the temperature is over ninety degrees, I alter my sessions. I try to work dogs in the morning and in the evening. No more than fifteen minutes or so of mobile work outside and lots of stay time in the shade. Dogs are given frequent water breaks. Depending upon the breed, the dog can be severely affected by extremely high temperatures. Dogs do not have porous skin—hence their intense panting in hot weather; they can have difficulty breathing in these conditions. I often will do up to fifty percent of a session inside during these heat spells. At times it is even recommended to stop training until the weather breaks.

The winter months can be rough, but the handler often has more difficulty than the dog. As far as training outside goes, most breeds can handle fairly frigid conditions, but single-digit and below-zero temperatures are times that a handler should work only briefly outside and instead concentrate on the commands inside. Due to the dog's inability to breath through its skin and possibly having a heavy coat of fur and/or other coats, dogs can handle the average time of a training session in the cold well. In the cold weather, try to keep the dog moving. Stays should not be incredibly long. If it is twenty degrees, I have seldom had difficulty in completing a normal session with most dogs. In the winter I recommend working the dog mid-day, if possible, because that is usually the warmest part of the day. During rain and snowstorms, I like to get the dogs out to work for at least five to ten minutes. Do realize that cars do not only drive on sunny days and balls do not only bounce across roads on fair weather days! Dogs need to be responsive regardless of the variables Mother Nature dishes out. A word of caution: DO NOT practice outside during thunder and lightening storms!

Summary of Key Points

🐾 When working with a dog in a one-on-one situation, the handler is dealing with the dog's natural rank.

🐾 A dog's social rank is determined by its peers or pack members.

🐾 Socially, there is always a ladder; there are never multiples of the same numbered rank in the dog's head.

🐾 A multi-alpha environment is a foreign concept to a dog.

🐾 Dogs ranked between three and six are usually the most obedient and preferred companions.

🐾 We deal with the human to canine relationship, not the canine to canine relationship.

🐾 No grabbing the scruff of the neck for any reprimanding.

🐾 Dogs and wolves learn and analyze their environment the same way.

🐾 Canines think very methodically—one thing at a time.

🐾 The two most important aspects to teaching a dog are a good learning environment and how the handler conducts him- or herself.

🐾 The leash is the handler's main tool, other than him- or herself, until respect is gained. The leash is a freedom stick, but try to not let it become a crutch.

🐾 Never give a correction without a command.

🐾 Treats and heavy-handed techniques are never used as a motivation.

🐾 Dogs are simple souls.

🐾 "Work" the dog, do not just put the dog through the motions.

🐾 Always give the dog something to think about—it creates a better learning environment.

🐾 A handler's physical presentation is really important to achieve success in dog training. Make sure to practice with the invisible dog, Fred, while the Checklist is learned.

🐾 Being a keen observer makes a person a great handler and owner.

🐾 Love creates safety, security, comfort, and happiness.

🐾 Respect is the working element of the relationship. Through giving good guidance, you achieve responsiveness. This is a mutually respectful relationship.

❧ You must walk a fine line between being compassionate and firm; you never should teeter more than 45% to 55% one way or the other.

❧ Trust is a feeling that develops as respect is earned by the handler. The dog should trust the handler more than the handler trusts the dog.

❧ When it comes to a training timetable, remember to be patient—dogs do not have deadlines.

❧ Quality more than quantity: practice in short but frequent sessions.

❧ Rough play is good—just avoid having the dog become frenzied. Avoid rough play if the dog is trying to physically dominate you.

❧ Dogs can withstand the cold most times, but the summer heat is where the real danger usually lies.

Canine Instinct's Foundation

Building Blocks

Every canine that is going to learn needs to start off with a foundation. Canine Instinct's building blocks are its basic obedience commands: **sit, stay, down, come, heel, take-a-break,** and **no**. Concepts of boundary training are usually incorporated into my basic obedience training, unless it is not applicable. When working with dogs please realize that they do not have deadlines. People have deadlines for dogs sometimes, but dogs do not have deadlines. We want to teach dogs in plateaus, meaning that once a canine understands one concept, the handler should allow for time where the canine only does things right. If the dog is quickly forced to learn a new command/concept to move on to the next thing, often it is not given enough time to acknowledge what is right and what is wrong. Typically, I start teaching a dog at four months of age or older. We will be breaking down these commands individually to illustrate the operations of how Canine

Instinct executes them.

Training Devices

The training equipment that I use is as follows: a six-foot lead, a twenty-foot lead, a fifty-foot lead, a body harness, a Halti (this is a head harness that aids in controlling a canine's muzzle), a regular flat collar, and a chain collar. The six-foot lead is used throughout training to assist in all commands. The twenty-foot lead is used for stays and recalls up to twenty feet away from the handler. This lead is also used during *freestyle* training segments, which are explained later in this chapter. The fifty-foot lead is used for stays and recalls up to fifty feet away from the handler. The body harness is used with dogs weighing approximately fifteen pounds and under for training, instead of a collar, because I feel that I can physically control the dog more safely and efficiently. The Halti is used with big, strong, unruly dogs that do not walk well on a leash. Some dogs that warrant the Halti feel uncomfortable with it on and with its use—therefore, it cannot be used on them. I find that a handler is better able to use the Halti when the dog has a grasp of the commands, rather than with the dog learning on the Halti from scratch. Sometimes, when the dog is aware of what is happening with the training, he or she does not stress out over wearing the Halti. *Do not force this apparatus upon a dog.* The regular flat collar is the collar that a canine wears all the time. In training, it is used any time the twenty- or fifty-foot leads are used. The chain collar is used when working a dog on the six-foot lead, especially with the heel command. This device is often called the choke collar; it can be as such, if placed on a canine one of two ways. The choke way is incorrect. Used the correct way, it is called a slip collar. The chain collars that I use are considered medium thickness. The lightweight collar provides more control. The heavier collars are too bulky, and corrections are not as good with these collars. See pictures to see the proper way to place the chain collar.

With dog in front of you, place chain on correctly this way.

This is the wrong way to put the chain on a dog.

On Lead and Off Lead

This is a judgment call on the handler's behalf. There are some breeds that I would never trust off lead because of their personalities and hearsay (i.e., "bad stories"). Other dogs have no opportunity to be off lead because they live in an urban environment. If I am going to be walking through town with my dogs, I have them on lead because it is the safest thing to do. My dogs do not even wear a collar, unless they are working, but urban environments always pose extra danger to dogs. For those of you who wish to take the risk of off-lead work with your dog, it is a completely different ball game but with the same rules, as when the dog was on lead in all environments. Often the handler has to be twice as much on top of things due to the lack of physical control of which that the canine is totally aware. A dog should only work with the come command off lead if its work is consistently flawless on lead for at least a few weeks. If a dog makes any mistakes off lead, it should immediately be placed on lead again. This makes the dog aware that it clearly has to earn every moment off lead by performing perfectly. This is a game of give and take, through trial and error. I never start with off-lead work before at least one solid month or more of good work on lead. Off-lead work is very advanced obedience, which requires the handler to relay body language to the dog for communication. Good luck and use your freedom stick when needed!

Follow the Leader

I love this exercise! It is very simple and I do not know of anyone who does this kind of exercise in the way I will be explaining, at least in my area of the country. *Follow the leader* is an attention-getting exercise. The more attention the canine is giving you, the more the canine will be more responsive to you. Follow the leader can be done while walking and when standing still. This activity is done with a six-foot long leash. I will do this exercise at the beginning of an obedience session or during a session when the dog loses focus. While doing follow the leader, the canine is allowed to be at either your left or right side or behind you. You should walk at a fairly slow pace and occasionally give very calm praise. You should change direction frequently, making sure to turn abruptly and clearly in a direction. No tentative steps should be taken or meandering done. This way, despite the spontaneity, the guidance is very clear. The more direction is changed, the more the dog is forced to pay attention.

If the dog does not follow your lead when you turn, wait until you feel tension on the leash, then give a quick tug and release correction, followed with saying, "This way." Do not say "This way" as you make a turn—this is a frequent mistake. Let the dog learn to fully pay attention to you by not giving verbal hints. When the dog has not made any mistakes after a minute or so, then it is a good idea to stop and bend down to give him or her praise and acknowledgment for his or her compliance, then proceed with this concept again. The dog will be even more attentive because you have given him or her approval for recently good actions. You will notice that the dog should basically be matching your speed if it is in an acceptable position. When you stop, the dog should stop as well; if the dog goes in front of you, then give a quick tug and release and remain silent. When the dog notices you are stationary, he or she will stop and eventually sit. This exercise should be done for at least a few minutes when in use. Remaining silent while giving a tug and release as necessary makes the dog aware that it should not pull on the leash whether or not you are in motion.

Follow the leader is also an excellent exercise for the handler because it forces the handler to avoid concentrating on what the dog is doing by not looking at the dog. Since humans are such visually oriented creatures, when we simultaneously handle a canine and look at it, we tend to focus on the dog's actions as opposed to our own. The handler should not be looking at the dog while doing this exercise other than when bending down to give praise. Many of my clients like to use a follow the leader walk in place of the heel because eventually the dogs will place themselves in a relaxed heel position and be more compliant because it is essentially on a *take-a-break*. Wonderful concept!

Sit

This is a very simple command. *Sit* is a position meaning the dog's hind end is on the ground. The front half of the dog's body is upright, with its front legs straight and its paws on the ground. The hand signal used for sit is the backside of the hand. Until the dog is performing the command flawlessly, both the physical and verbal command should be given at the same time so the dog knows that they mean the same thing. This should be done with all commands that have hand signals. Later on, the handler can use either command. Sit is used in conjunction with come, heel, and stay. People often misuse this command. People often tell the dog to sit, and when the dog gets up, they place the dog back in the same spot and say, "Sit." This immediately associates sit with duration of time, which is wrong.

As simple as it seems, this command can give a handler tremendous difficulty because the sit position is not a very natural one. The only time wolves really sit is when they are performing the classic howl and when observing their environment. I place the dog in a sit with other commands to gain control and when I want it to observe the environment. The sit is used mainly on a sit-stay. Wolves eat lying down or standing. They hunt standing or crouching down, and they sleep lying down. Since the sit position is an infrequent occurrence in nature, in comparison to other positions, the canine can be resistant to do it, especially dominant and mature canines.

A handler, at times, will have to earn a certain level of respect with other commands prior to executing the sit command effectively. I use sit when heeling with the canine. When the handler stops, the canine should be taught to sit. The sit is also used with the stay command and the come command. If the dog does not sit, then the handler can make it sit by gently lifting the muzzle up while pushing down on the hips at the same time. There should be little to no force involved. Making a sit happen should be mechanical—any physically negative connotations of a forced sit should be avoided. If the dog does not want the handler to touch its muzzle, then the handler can pull back and down on the leash so there is no contact with the dog's mouth. If the dog gives the handler a hard time by stepping away from the handler when the handler is trying to get the dog to sit, then the leash should be held at the base, near the collar, in one spot, with the right hand. Then the handler's left hand should push down on the dog's left hip to make its hind end go down. This may take a while, but as the handler you should stick with it. I have seen a handler's entire progress reach a premature peak due to inconsistent sitting behavior on the dog's behalf. This is quite common because the handler often does not view the sit as a big deal; however, most of the time the dog does. Therefore, the dog will not be as responsive as it should in other areas being worked.

Basically, there are two techniques to get the dog to sit when the dog continuously refuses to do so. The first technique we take up is from the heel position since that is the most common position to be in when telling the dog to sit; however, this technique can be used from any handler position. The handler comes to a stop and the dog stops. The handler rotates his or her body at the hips, showing the dog the backside of the right hand, which is the hand signal for sit. With the handler's left hand low on the leash, the handler gives a quick tug and release, saying "Sit" at the same time. Now this does not guarantee that the dog will sit—that is what the other technique is for. The handler should try to get the dog to sit with the first technique because it requires less work. The second technique must also be done from the heel position if the handler is not there already. The handler will take his or her right hand and place it where the left hand was on the leash. The handler's left hand will go to the dog's left hip, so the dog cannot scoot out away from the handler. Then the handler will push down on the natural angle of the dog's back, saying "sit" at the same time. See pictures for assistance.

*Handler using the first technique. The Sit command hand
signal is showing the dog the backside of your hand, while
the handler is positioned at the dog's right side.*

Handler using the second technique.

Stay

This is the most valuable command that every canine needs to know—and know well. This command is the foundation of all of my teaching. My stay teaches a dog patience, to absorb its environment, and to make the handler the number one priority within that environment. A stay can be used as a teaching tool, a form of a time-out, a safety technique, and for mental collection. Sounds pretty good, right? Now how do you do it? This is the easiest command to teach. The number one reason why peoples' dogs do not stay well is because it takes time on the handler's behalf. A dog is not going to stay for ten minutes unless it is made to do so.

The black and white rule is very simple. Place the dog on a sit, then on a stay, and if he or she gets up, place him or her back in the same spot and repeat saying, "sit-stay." *Dogs can only make as big of a deal out of something as the handler does.* Regardless of the dog's performance, the handler should always remain collected. If you become upset in any way, it just emphasizes a lack of control to the canine. It is always helpful to know what the dog is thinking because then the handler can better correct the dog in the sense of where the handler will place him or herself in the environment. I always place the dog on a sit-stay. Never a down-stay because I do not want it to feel submissive, and never a stand-stay because all the dog has to do is take a step and it has made a mistake. The canine is allowed to lie down on his or her own; it is a more comfortable and natural position. I allow my dogs to spin three hundred and sixty degrees as long as their butts remain in the spot where I put them! Once the dog has laid down, it can sit up as well. To sum up, as long as the dog's butt is in the same spot where I placed it and it never leaves the ground, I do not mind what the dog does. The handler will accomplish every thing he or she needs to and more by doing the command this way. By allowing the dog to these latitudes, it is usually more willing to work with the handler. The canine absorbs much by taking advantage of the benefits allowed; because of this, the handler becomes a priority over everything that it absorbs in its environment. My backyard obedience dog (the family dog that most dogs are in our lives, as I call it), will always stay longer than my obedience test dog (one that completes organized tests with strict rules) that is not allowed to relax, absorb, and get comfortable, so that it eventually breaks the stay or remains stressed. A twenty to thirty minute stay with any and all distractions very often is my basic obedience goal. If the dog can do that, it will do anything well.

I can tell a person how well or poorly their dog will do by how well it stays or does not stay. A stay teaches a canine the norms within a given environment. This is the time that the canine learns about our world. The dogs have to teach themselves just as much as we teach them, and they do it on a stay.

If the handler knows what is going on in the dog's head, the handler can give the optimum correction. For example, if the canine breaks the stay, let's say three or more times, clearly there is a problem. This could be due to several things: the dog might not understand what to do, it might not want to do it, or it might be holding something else in the environment as its main priority. In any case, you should note that *distance equals less control* and the canine is fully aware of this fact. In the early stages when the novice handler lacks respect, the dog takes advantage of the handler. Often, when a handler goes to distance him or her from the dog, it will stand up and sometimes move. When the handler goes to correct the dog, by placing it back on a sit-stay, the dog immediately breaks it. Rather than getting pulled into this game or a "peeing contest," the handler should quickly end this turmoil.

I find that placing myself in the heel position, standing straight up, and saying, "sit-stay" assertively gets the best results in the most expedient fashion. Most of the time my sit-stay and back away works well, but do try what I just mentioned if all else fails. Just do not allow the dog to walk all over you. If you need to change the game to something else, quickly go into a very controlled heel to change the subject. It is important to see the situation through the dog's eyes. How a dog views its environment is quite different from how humans view it. The immediate area around the canine is its environment and *everything outside of that immediate area are subenvironments of the dog's environment.* Think of these subenvironments (activities and objects of any sort) as movies. Canines always have to be the main actors and actresses. They always have to be part of the best movie happening. They see it and go! What my stay does is take them off the movie screen and place them in the audience. This makes the canine see what he or she never saw before because the dog is always on the go and therefore unable to absorb its environment.

Stay can be broken down into three mental stages: the *alert stage, the absorbing stage,* and *the relaxed stage.* The first stage, the alert stage, is when the dog is first placed on a sit-stay. In this stage, the dog tries to anticipate when you are going to call it to come. Often the dog looks right at you throughout this entire stage. It is vital not to allow the canine to anticipate you. In this stage, if the dog breaks the stay, over ninety-nine percent of the time the dog will go to you. The majority of the time this is a short stage; however, dogs that are insecure often will linger in this stage longer than others.

The second stage, the absorbing stage, is the most dangerous phase of a stay. This is when the dog absorbs its environment and all the distractions within it. This is usually the longest stage. You must be aware of everything happening within the environment. You should know where the dog's mind is at all times. If, while absorbing its environment, the dog appears to be making a priority shift from you to a distraction within its environment, you must reposition yourself between the dog and the distraction, to break that focus. Occasionally, talking to the dog in this stage helps because if the dog will not make an effort to look in your direction then that is the time for you to reposition yourself to reduce the distance between yourself and the dog. If the dog breaks the stay in this stage it will go toward the most interesting stimulus within its environment. You may be that stimulus; however, most of the time you are not. This is when the dog learns how much it can physically move on a stay to fully absorb its environment. With each stay that passes within a given working session, this stage will become shorter and shorter because the dog has already absorbed its environment, with the exception of any newly introduced distractions.

The last stage, the relaxed stage, is when the dog lies down to become more comfortable and has accepted your role within the environment. If the dog breaks the stay in this stage it will, nine out of ten times, go toward you, in an apparent plea to do something else. The other ten percent of the time the dog will move to a new stimulus that has been introduced into the environment. Usually the handler has plenty of time to react physically and verbally because the dog is fairly sedate upon discovery of the distraction. These are the three stages that all dogs go through mentally when they are placed on a stay. I have seen dogs take over a half hour to go from stage one to stage three—others do it in a few minutes. It is of great benefit to you as a handler if you can acknowledge which mental stage of the stay the dog is in.

Other than the fearful canine, most dogs learn through trial and error, as mentioned earlier. In the majority of cases, for instance, if a dog is afraid of a horse it is usually due to a bad experience, such as getting kicked or chased. The average dog does not stop outside the paddock and observe what potentially dangerous creatures horses are prior to an experience with one. Not all dogs will evaluate a horse in this way; once they know my stay, however, they will be much more aware of their environment in the way that I would like them to be. When a dog is on a stay, it forces him or her to physically remain still, so you can encourage *maximum mental motion*. The stay is the only time that you can truly guarantee the dog is thinking about things the way you want. Once the canine has learned stay to a high degree of obedience, it will view everything as one environment that the handler is in control of. Until you reach that level of success, it is important to spend as little time as possible inside the canine's immediate environment, where it feels it has control.

My physical presentation to the canine in attempting this command is as follows: start from the heel position, at left, which is a very common predecessor to the stay command. Before stepping away from the dog, give the verbal and physical command. Showing the dog the open palm of your hand is the hand signal for stay. My first step away from the dog is in front of the dog. This is for two reasons: if the dog is going to get up and go, this position will stop the initial momentum and you are immediately presenting your body language to the canine by facing him or her. It is important to give the dog body language. This emphasizes for the dog the handler's control over the environment. You should always face the canine. Look in the direction of the dog to let it know that you have mental tabs on it. However, early in training, do not make eye contact because this will only encourage a mistake because the dog will be looking for a way out of its stay. Slowly distance yourself. Dogs do not like change, but if done slowly, they are more likely to accept it. As you distance yourself, never turn your back to the dog. If the dog is on the short leash (which it should be in the beginning), work your way out to the end of the leash, walk to what I refer to as the "bottom half of the clock." That is, consider the dog is in the center of a clock; at the end of the leash you are standing at six o'clock, facing the dog. Walk slowly back and forth from three o'clock to nine o'clock. Once the dog can comply with this movement several times, then continue this movement farther and farther away.

The purpose of the clock movements is to establish that stay is not a game of freeze, or who can stay longer. This is a very important concept. At this point if you are not going to give the dog a take-a-break or a come command, then work yourself back toward the dog the exact same way you worked your way out, by reversing your movements. Throughout exercising the stay command, only talk to the canine occasionally to let it know you are watching and you are in control. Give words of praise such as "good boy" or "good girl," its name, "good job," etc. It is important to create only brief, occasional conversation, for two reasons: first, if you are constantly talking to the dog, it will be looking at you most of the time. What is wrong with that? Remember a stay is when a dog absorbs its environment and makes the handler its number one priority through absorption of the environment. The canine cannot be absorbing its environment to the highest degree when it is looking at the handler. The second reason is that if you continually talk to the dog and nothing happens, then it will flip you the paw and ignore you when you want its attention to come. The canine will say to itself, "That dope calls my name and praises me constantly, then makes me remain in one spot! Well forget him!" So only talk to the dog once in a while, when he or she is on a stay.

If the dog breaks the stay, as you work your way away from it, immediately say "sit-stay" and give the hand signal. I do not necessarily expect the canine to sit-stay. At the very least it should get you on the dog's mind, which should allow you to move in and physically correct the dog. To understand the stay command can be complex for a canine, but to teach it should be relatively simple. The number one reason why people's dogs do not stay is because they do not take the time to teach the dog the stay. Make sure to practice this command in any environment that the dog is allowed in so that you become a priority over everything within those environments. Follow all these instructions within those environments to desensitize the dog so only newly introduced situations or objects are potential problems. One of my adages is "a five-minute stay per day keeps the headaches away." If a handler places a dog on a five-minute stay one time each day for one month in a difficult setting, then that dog will stay exceptionally well (and listen well overall). See pictures for assistance.

When first teaching the stay command, on and off lead, the handler should not walk completely around the dog. After a few weeks of working on lead and later off lead, it is good for the handler to walk completely around the dog to teach it to what degree it can move while on a stay. However, early on we do not want to put any more stress on the dog than necessary by walking behind it, creating discomfort.

The handler starts with the dog on his left side, with the dog in a sit position.

Stay. Come. Heel. Every Time.

The handler shows and tells the dog to sit.

The handler shows and tells the dog to stay.

Stay. Come. Heel. Every Time.

The handler's first step directly in front of the dog.

Canine Instinct's Foundation.

*The handler walks straight back away from the dog
to the end of the lead.*

*The handler walks the bottom half of
the clock to three o'clock.*

*The handler walks the bottom half of the
clock to nine o'clock.*

Come

This command involves the dog moving from a distant
point to a controlled sit position, in front of the
handler. Please start off teaching on a six-foot leash
and wait until the dog is consistently doing well before
practicing on a longer leash. Start teaching this command when the dog is on a sit-stay. When you are
going to use this command, you should get the dog's
attention prior to giving the command. You can do this
by saying the dog's name and/or saying words of praise.
Most of the time whatever a dog is looking at is what
it is thinking about when stimulated at any level.

Sometimes insecure and uncomfortable dogs will look at everything but what they are thinking about.

Give the dog a second to look in your direction, then say "come." At the same time, give the hand signal, which is a slap of the hand on the thigh. This is when you want to give constant praise to the canine from start to finish. This keeps the canine focused on you to complete the task. Say "Let's go," "You can do it," "Good boy," "Good girl," anything but the command itself. If a dog just sits still when called, you should give a tug and release on the leash and repeat the command. Only reel in a dog if absolutely necessary.

To encourage a dog to respond more crisply, you both use and not use the advantage of your physical height. All wolves are relatively the same height, while humans are naturally taller, which makes us naturally more physically domineering to the dog. By squatting to the dog's level, you can be more physically inviting. When the dog gets to you on the recall, you can stand up with the dog's muzzle in the palm of your hand while pushing down on its hips. If able it would be best to exercise option one of the "sit" followed by option two of the "sit" if necessary, as our initial attempt on the finish of the recall. In this way you are going from a low crouching level, a friendly height, to a standing position, which is more authoritarian. If the dog is moving around a lot, then use the two different techniques for the sit, as explained previously.

What else can you do when the dog is moving toward you? You can take a few steps away from the dog, enticing it to pick up its speed and complete the command close to you, as planned. When the dog moves off the beaten path on a recall, you should take a giant step in the opposite direction that the dog went. At the same time, repeat the come command and give a quick tug and release on the leash. Once the dog is back on the beaten path, you should square back up to the original position and location that you called the dog from and finish the recall. Make sure to give the dog praise from the time it leaves point A, until it gets to point B, you. Be sure to keep the dog in front of you when it is in motion. You should use your body like a funnel, by holding your arms out and guiding the dog to the proper come position. When the canine reaches you, make it sit facing you within arms' reach. Never walk toward the canine when it is on a recall. Usually when you approach a canine on a recall it is because the dog is hesitating toward the latter part of the recall. Since the dog is already questioning the desired action that you want, you should not approach the dog as it is likely to shy away from you at this point. Please do not forget the sit, to complete the task. I often see a handler so excited because the dog actually came that the handler forgets all about the sit. The sit is just as important as the recall itself. I could tell you countless stories where the handler calls the dog and it comes, only to go right by the handler. Come is helpful only if the canine actually comes close to the handler. The sit command helps the handler keep a lid on the situation.

When using a long lead, the handler should stand on the same side of the lead as the dog. Otherwise the dog may step on the lead. Once the dog has progressed to where the handler is doing long recalls with the six-foot lead, the handler should place the lead behind or to the side of the dog so it does not step on the lead. If the dog goes in the wrong direction, the handler should immediately grab the lead and say, "come" and give a tug on the lead; if the dog does not comply, it should be reeled into the handler, by repeating the continual tugs and releases as you say "come."

When the dog starts the off-lead work, you should set up the environment in such a way that the dog understands you have control. You do not want to place a dog in a location within an environment that makes you vulnerable.

Down

I find that my method of teaching down is exceptionally unique. It depends on the individual dog as to whether it is viewed as a submissive position or not. The time at which the command is given can often affect how the dog views the down position. I try to avoid making the dog feel submissive to me as much as possible. With my dogs I never really *make* them lie down. To me it makes absolutely no difference whether the dog is lying down or not. I always allow the dog to lie down, if it wants to. It certainly is more comfortable than sitting. The position of down is when all four legs of the dog are flat on the ground. The dog learns what this word means, by me letting it know what it is doing any time the dog goes into the down position. By introducing the concept of down in this fashion, it minimizes any dominate versus submissive relation-ship. The dog simply views the situation as both itself and the handler getting what they want; therefore, it is a positive experience. In time the dog will lie down happily whenever the handler wants it to because this command has never been forced upon it. If the dog is resistant to this command down the road, then I simply will not use it. It is not worth harming the relationship.

When the dog lies down, I will say "down" followed by praise. Simultaneously, I will give the hand signal for down. I hold my arm out toward the dog with a closed fist. Often this command is taught when the dog is on a stay that is moving into the relaxed stage; therefore, the handler needs to say "stay" after giving a down command. This last command is given because, as mentioned earlier, the last thing the handler says is the last thing the dog remembers. Do not dwell on this command; it is the least important. I do not even include it in my basic obedience programs anymore. This command is not in the Checklist at the end of this chapter because of its overall insignificance. See picture for the hand signal.

*Showing the dog a closed fist is the hand
signal for the down command.*

Heel

Handler coordination is a must for all canine handling, but with the heel command it is life and death! I teach "Heel" to mean *at left*—the command is a *position*. Regardless of the handler's speed while in motion, the dog should always be on the left side when this command is in effect. Despite variations in speed, the overall pace of the walk should be slow. Using the left hand, the handler should always have a hold as low as possible on the leash, knuckles up and palm down. Often with large dogs the handler is holding just above the metal clasp at the base of the leash. The dog will feel the correction immediately when given due to the hand position on the leash. Do make sure not to create any tension on the leash other than at times of correction. A relaxed leash equals a relaxed dog. The dog's front legs should never be more than one foot out to the side away from the handler's left leg. What has been mentioned thus far about the heel is the physical positioning of the handler in relationship to the dog; this positioning never changes.

Next are the attention-getting components of the heel command—how to get and maintain the dog in the heel position. The heel command has a simple formula: when the handler stops, the dog sits, in the heel position. When the handler resumes walking, the dog does the same, at the handler's pace. The correction for heel works on *a tug and release system*. Any time the handler needs to give a correction because the canine is not in the heel position, the handler should give a quick tug on the leash, say "heel," and immediately relax the leash. This correction should happen in a fraction of a second. Each correction is a pulsating-like tug, either a flick of the wrist or a bend at the elbow, nothing more. When the handler pulls on the leash, the dog often tenses up and freezes, or pulls even more. The leash should only be tense for a fraction of a second, as mentioned. The leash might be tense frequently in the beginning, but each correction should be very quick. To minimize constant corrections, the handler should stop often. I would say to stop every twenty to forty feet, on average, until the canine greatly improves. The handler can, and at times should, stop more frequently than recommended. The more the handler stops, the more aware the dog is of the handler's physical location. In conjunction with stopping often, the handler should do many inside turns, which are left-handed turns toward the dog. Turns should be done sharply in a U-shaped pattern. For the first few weeks the handler should only do inside turns because when the handler turns to the left, he or she physically walks in front of the canine. This gets the canine's attention, passively but physically forcing the dog to turn with the handler. I recommend that the handler come to a stop once the turn is completed. When the dog's body is parallel and aligned with the handler's body, the handler should stop, because the handler has changed the canine's direction one hundred eighty degrees, slowing its momentum nearly to a stop—thus the handler is essentially setting the dog up for success. Before the handler stops during a turn, the handler should talk with the dog, to encourage it to look up at him or her. If the handler can get the dog's attention, since usually what a dog looks at is what it is thinking about, the likelihood of the dog performing well should increase. *Do* give praise to the dog when walking. Because a good deal of coordination is involved with the heel command, many handlers remain mostly silent while walking. The canine *must* hear words of encouragement when he or she is not getting corrected. Using only words of correction does not keep the atmosphere positive. *Do* be sure to never give a correction without giving a command. This happens more with the heel command than any other command. Every time the handler stops, the dog should immediately stop, then sit in the heel position within a second. Often, early on, some dogs will continue to walk when the handler stops. As soon as the dog takes one step ahead of the handler, the dog should immediately be placed back in the heel position. The handler should say "heel" followed by "sit." Since dogs learn through trial and error, it is important to allow them to go through the decision-making process; however, when the second a mistake is made, the proper correction should be applied. While the handler is stationary during the heel command, the dog should be sitting at the handler's left side. If the dog gets up on its own, the handler should place the canine back in the heel position, and then say "sit-stay," and make the dog sit-stay. The dog must not be confused between sit and stay—each word clearly has its own meaning that does not interfere with any other commands. If the handler places the dog in the heel position and just says "Sit," then the handler is implying that sit and stay have the same meaning. The handler needs to give the right command at the right time. Sometimes the canine will take a side step away from the handler and then face him or her. Dogs do this when they feel they can get away with it. The canine wants to see the handler's face because that is where his or her emotional presentation is commonly displayed.

As the weeks go by and the dog improves with its obedience, the handler can incorporate outside turns, right-handed turns away from the dog, along with continual changes in walking speed. The changing of speed is a more advanced technique. I use it to help keep the canine focused on the handler. The same goes for outside turns (additionally, it is not always practical to turn to the left). Outside turns should also be done *in a very sharp U-shaped pattern*. When turning to the right, the handler should talk to the dog and tap his or her leg while turning. On a right turn there is no physical barrier telling the canine to turn. All the dog sees are distractions; the handler is *out of sight, out of mind*. Giving a correction at the right time on a right-handed turn is very important. If the middle of the bend of a U-turn is labeled as twelve o'clock, the handler should never give a correction prior to twelve o'clock because if the handler tugs on the leash the handler will pull the dog into the back of his or her leg. When the handler gives a correction to the dog after they have walked to twelve o'clock, the dog will then be tugged more toward the handler's left side because the handler is not walking away from the dog from that point on.

If the handler does a sharp U-shaped pattern, then at most there should only be two corrections. The wider the turns, the more corrections the handler will have to make, because the dog has more time to make mistakes and the handler's guidance is not fully understood. If the handler has waited until the proper time to introduce this concept of the U-shaped pattern, to the dog, it comes with ease. Since the canine can only think of one thing at a time, the canine must always pay attention to the handler. The ideal handler is able to keep the dog's mind on the go almost all the time when performing the heel command. I often tell my clients to think of the heel concept as a *mental race*. If the handler is giving the canine things to do at the rate at which it can process them, then the dog will perform perfectly. If the handler is giving the canine things to do slower than at the rate at which the canine can think, then it will be thinking about the things that it wants to think about (which will not be heeling). If the handler is giving the canine things to do faster than the rate at which it can think, then its work load will slow the canine down a great deal (we want to avoid this as well; however, I will do this with egotistical canines). See pictures and diagrams for assistance.

These are all patterns that I commonly use in the first several weeks of teaching the dog. Notice I have only drawn the handler and dog turning to the left. Frequent stops are stressed, while heeling, to get and maintain the dog's attention. Try to make many of your turns U-shaped, nice and sharp-not C-shaped. Once the dog is heeling nicely, the handler can make these patterns to the right as well. Refer to the chapter titled "My Approach to the Canine," section on communicating with the canine, where I talk about a handler's structure, for any explanations.

The handler standing with the dog in the heel position. Note the placement of the handler's left arm, left hand, leash, and left leg in relationship to the dog.

Stay. Come. Heel. Every Time.

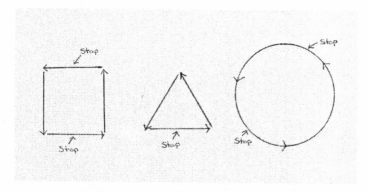

*Walking in squares, triangles, and circles are
easy patterns and provide practice for a variety
of important angles on the turns and stops.*

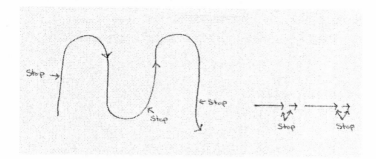

*Walking in a continual "S" pattern and "I"
pattern focuses on turns and stops.*

On the outside turn, the handler should only correct
the dog from twelve o'clock and after. Prior to twelve
o'clock, all corrections result in placing the canine
into the back of the handler's leg. Correcting after
twelve o'clock will place the dog in the proper heel
position.

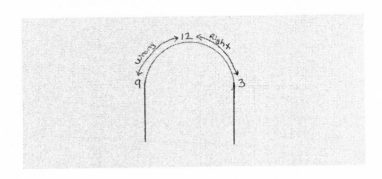

Walking the top perimeter of a clock, on a "U"-turn.

When a dog sits perpendicular to the handler, while on a heel, the handler immediately does a tight inside circle with the dog and stops at his original position. If done well, this correction almost always aligns the dog's body parallel and even to the handler's body.

This is a four-step breakdown of correcting the dog's perpendicular position to an appropriate parallel position (the heel position). This process should take one to three seconds to complete.

When a dog sits behind the handler, while on a heel, the handler immediately takes one giant step forward (with the left leg) to get the dog to step forward. Then the handler quickly takes one giant step back with the same leg to the original position. At this time, the dog should be parallel and even with the handler.

This is a four-step breakdown of correcting the dog for stopping behind the handler out of the heel position. This should correct the dog's position behind to position alongside the handler. This process should take no more than a second to complete.

Take-a-Break

This is the canine's favorite command—it relieves the canine of its duties. It means to "do whatever you want within reason." I teach this from a stay, and move the dog from the stay by giving a quick tug and release on the leash while saying "take-a-break," to let the dog know that it is all right to move freely now. When giving the command I move my arms from across my chest to an arms-open position; this is the hand signal for take-a-break. I then move in any direction away from the dog to entice it to follow. I like to praise the dog when giving this command so that the dog thinks of it pleasurably. It also lets the dog know that it is OK to essentially be breaking a stay. A novice handler usually has no trouble with this one. See picture for hand signal.

The handler starts with arms close to the body.

*The handler opens arms wide, showing the
dog the take-a-break hand signal.*

Freestyle

Mixing the circle of fun with the circle of obedience is
attempted in what I refer to as *freestyle*. Freestyle is
done with a twenty-foot lead. All the commands can
be used during freestyle teaching with the exception of
the heel command. Follow the Leader is a good
exercise to do prior to a freestyle session. This is the
intermediate stage between on lead and off lead. Trust
is a major factor in freestyle. The handler plays with
the dog but frequently uses commands to let the dog
know that it has to listen regardless of its frame of
mind, or the activities and environment at hand. If the

dog is disobedient, then the long lead is on the dog to make the dog do the command, reinforcing the *first time told, second time fixed* concept.

Freestyle should always be fun and upbeat. The atmosphere should be very light. This is when to blend play and obedience; it also helps the canine realize that it can listen and be happy at the same time. The handler should see if he or she could keep the dog's attention without giving commands. This makes the handler aware of the dog's priorities. Give lots of conversational praise. Physically gesture to the dog that you are fun and exciting: bend down low and move your arms around a little bit, saying something like "Lets go..." or "Over here"! If the dog comes to you, then give it a pat on the side and send it on its way.

This exercise is a great time to figure out the body language that will give you as a handler the edge when exercising commands. Example: if the dog comes over to you when you bend down low, then you most definitely want to bend down low when you use the come command. It is extremely important that roughly two-thirds of the time you are playing with the dog and roughly one-third of the time you are having the dog execute commands. The work time should be infused throughout the entire session. Example: if you do freestyle for three minutes, then a total of one minute out of the entire three minutes is work time. This keeps the atmosphere spontaneous and fun—and focuses the dog's attention.

This ratio is critical. Any more than one-third work time makes most dogs feel like they are in a formal work session—and they should be viewing it as informal and fun! Essentially, the dog is being placed in a mind-set where you have the least control, to establish control. You are making the dog like a switch...on/off.

Toys can be used in freestyle. Example: place dog on a stay, throw a ball, then give a take-a-break and fetch it up! The next few throws just let the dog go get the ball, then try a stay again before throwing the ball. This exercise strengthens the relationship between dog and handler. Remember, brief stays, lots of play, and spontaneity. Enjoy!

Boundary Training

The way in which I teach a canine its home boundaries is very simple. I use the stay command in a different context. I will start to teach a dog its boundaries after it has gained enough respect for the handler and has sufficient knowledge to do the stay command well. When introducing this concept, I am often about four to six weeks into the training. First choose the boundaries. It is best to use physical landmarks for the boundary lines—this could be a flag, tree, stonewall, grass to pavement or to forest—anything that stands out. These kinds of objects are helpful to canines. I would say that canines can learn the boundary concepts up to twice as fast if physical landmarks are used. Dogs that do not have landmarks tend to remain far away from the boundary lines. They stay near the middle of the allowed area in order to play it safe.

The process of teaching a canine this is as follows.

Work with only one area until the dog has mastered the concept of the boundary training; the other areas will then come with ease. Determine the boundary line. To give a correction, the canine must cross the line. When the dog does cross the line, you should place the dog back on the proper side and say "stay" and give the hand signal. As introduction to the boundaries, you can use follow the leader. By doing so, you are able to turn around and give the dog a stay correction as you scurry or pull the dog back into the permitted area. Since follow the leader is a "take-a-break" walk, the dog is allowed to follow you. If you give a heel or come command through the boundary, and follow it with a correction, then you are hurting the obedience relationship.

Once the dog has the boundary concept understood with follow the leader, then practice on the long lead as seen in the diagrams. Do not place the dog on a sit-stay. Just tell the dog to stay, and make sure it is on the proper side of the boundary line. *Do not* say "no," or anything else for that matter, only "stay." It is very common for the canine to place itself on a sit-stay because that is how the dog knows to stay. If the dog sits, then walk back and forth on the wrong side saying "take-a-break" with lots of praise. If the dog crosses the line again, give the stay command and place the dog on the proper side. Go back and forth from the proper side to the wrong side praising and playing with the dog the entire time. Any time the canine makes a mistake, just place it back within the boundary lines. This is an example of taking advantage of the concept that *the dog will never do more than what the handler makes it do* and knowing that the dog will probably break the stay and eventually go in the direction of the allowed area. Make sure to praise the canine when it reacts in the way you desire.

Using toys works well in boundary training. Throw the toy several times into the allowed area and then into the bad area. When the dog *crosses* the line, say "stay" and correct the dog. Placing distractions on the bad side encourages the dog to cross the boundary lines. This action is *encouraged* so that you can *discourage* this action! You force the dog to learn through trial and error. When using a toy, make sure that the canine gets its fair share of "fun time" because you want the dog to think positively about the boundaries. Do not practice the boundaries more than ten minutes per day. This can be a very stressful exercise. If the canine is not trustworthy, then this should be introduced with a twenty-foot leash on the dog. In a month's time the dog should be doing very well with its boundary work. This boundary concept can be applied in the house, car, or place of work, as well as with entrances and exits. It is a wonderful safety device.

I have known handlers with dogs one year of age and under have nearly perfect results by working with this method. I have known people with dogs over a year of age have about an eighty percent success rate. There is a small percentage of canines that only make *their own* boundaries. These dogs need a physical barrier rather than a mental one. With canines that are taught using this method, every once in a while it is prudent to test them to refresh their memory of the rules. Lastly, it is important to do a formal stay after boundary training is over because we do not want the dog to get confused and think that the meaning of stay has changed (just a short formal stay). See pictures and diagrams for assistance.

My first recommendation is to start teaching the boundaries from the outside in. The handler should be outside of the boundaries and the dog should be inside the boundaries. The handler should move back and forth, side to side, while praising the dog doing follow the leader. This is an example of encouraging the mistake to discourage the mistake. We want to entice the dog to cross the line so we can place the dog back on the proper side. We can only correct the dog if it steps on or crosses the line. This is done for all boundary lines. It is very important to not give a correction until the dog actually steps on or across the boundary line. No matter how likely the dog seems ready to make a mistake, the handler must allow the dog to initiate a mistake.

Introduction to boundary training using follow the leader.

Introduction to boundary training using follow the leader. Crossing the boundary line using follow the leader.

Turning around to give the "stay!" correction to the dog that has crossed the boundary line.

Stay. Come. Heel. Every Time.

*The dog respecting the boundary line, despite the
handler pulling on the lead. The handler should
praise the dog when going to resist walking further.*

Once the dog is responding to the boundary corrections well, the handler can place the dog on the long lead and just run in and out of the boundaries, creating distractions for the dog. Make sure that the dog is allowed to engage with the distractions being used inside the boundary, to keep things positive.

When practicing the boundaries from the inside out, which is done after practicing from the outside in, the same rules apply. The handler must be inside the boundaries with the dog and there must be a stimulus on the outside of the boundaries that the dog is interested in. Toys, animals, people, cars, etc.—whatever is at the handler's disposal. It is important to practice from the inside out because it is a more realistic situation.

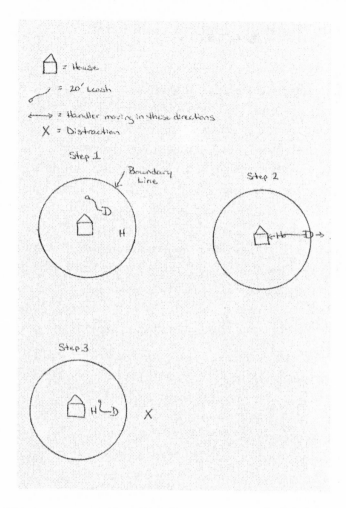

This is step one, where both the handler and dog are in the permitted area with the dog on a long lead. This is step two, where the dog goes for the distraction on the outside of the boundary and the handler pulls the dog back inside the line as the handler tells the dog "stay!" This is step three, where the dog runs after the distraction and comes to a complete stop on its own without any correction, inside the boundary.

The Negative Concept Command

The last basic obedience command deals with manners. Up to this point all commands should be viewed positively and the dog should learn them through gradual practice. The no command deals with negative concepts. With this command you discourage current behavior that you do not ever want the canine to do again. You want the dog to view this command negatively. You want the dog to say to itself, "This it is not worth doing." When correcting a canine with this command, you must do it quickly and crisply. Make sure that there is no eye contact, especially if the dog is going to feel bad, defensive, or offensive—none of which are good. So, *you do not want to make eye contact!* All three of these things could spike aggression.

You get the canine to view the negative concept command as purely negative by using a technique known as "flooding." This means constantly exposing the dog to these problem areas until they dissipate. To clearly get the proper message across to the canine that these behaviors are unacceptable, you must create "intentional" spontaneous situations—i.e., you should encourage the problem to discourage the problem. When you correct the dog for doing something bad and the situation never occurs again, then this is considered as being corrected in the short term because the consequence does not outweigh the reward. You need to return immediately to this "intentionally spontaneous" (or "imitation natural occurrence") and encourage the bad behavior several more times in a row to discourage the problem. By increasing the frequency of the situation, the consequence now weighs more heavily than the reward. Now the dog will view these corrections as long-term fixing corrections. Additionally, you should take roughly five-minute intervals to do nothing but *encourage the problem to discourage the problem*. Correcting problems this way will make the dog care about what you are dissatisfied with so it will make long-term changes in its presentation for the better. I certainly recommend doing most of this after the dog has learned the other commands well. It is important to understand that dogs see things as either good or bad. As mentioned earlier, they are grey creatures, but if they do not view something as bad then it is good to them.

No

This is the most overly used word in the canine dictionary. I only use this command when discouraging unwarranted barking, mouthing, destructiveness, jumping, and/or any aggressive behavior. This command also means to remove oneself from a being or an object that one is not supposed to be on. In regard to objects in general, it is a fairly easy concept. If the canine is on an object that it should not be on, simply say "no" and remove the dog immediately, usually taking hold of the dog's collar or coaxing the dog off the object. A handler might need to be a little more cautious with an aggressive dog. With a wary canine, coaxing is recommended rather then physically moving the dog. However, do remember that the leash is your friend and it is a very helpful tool in these situations.

Sometimes if a dog is stubborn about jumping on the counters and the tables, I will take a two-by-four stud, the length of the counter or table, and rest it on the edge of the object, just enough so that it will remain balancing on the counter or table. When the dog jumps up it will knock the stud down and usually not attempt this behavior again—or at least not too many more times. In addition to the stud, I will also take a soda can that has a few pennies in it, tape over the top, and place it on the stud. When the stud falls, the can will make an awful noise, scaring the dog. Do not use the can trick if there is concern that the dog may eat the can; otherwise, this is a safe and very effective method. If someone is present, then another trick that has had some success is taking a heavy book and dropping it on the floor, which makes a startling sound, potentially scaring the dog.

Jumping up on people can be much more difficult to correct. When discouraging this behavior, the handler takes a step toward the dog and brushes both front paws to one side, saying "no." This gives the dog an element of surprise, which most dogs dislike. Occasionally, dominant, stubborn canines get testy, or regard this as a game. The best thing to do with these dogs is to follow the procedure previously explained: continue to walk straight toward them for ten to fifteen feet, basically to the point where they are shying away from you. Dogs expect a human to stand still or back up when jumped upon—they do not anticipate the person to walk straight toward and into them!

What I absolutely do *not* do are kneeing in the chest, stepping on toes, or throwing the dog over backward. These get the message across; however, my methods work better on both a mental and a physical level. You want to make sure that the "first time told, second time fixed" concept is in operation, not just with no, but with all the commands. If the dog jumps on a person or objects in any way after being told to get off by you saying no, then repeat the process and then place the dog on a sit-stay (for a time-out) at a reasonable distance from temptation. If you are not having any jumping issues with the dog but others in the environment are, then show them what to do. A method to discourage the jumping when the dog is jumping on someone other than yourself is thread your forearm directly in front of the dog's hind legs and slightly elevate the dog's legs off the ground, pulling the dog away from its target. This is, of course, followed by a sit-stay (for a minute or so). See pictures and diagrams for assistance.

This command is not given when a dog breaks another command. It is best not to associate a negative concept with a positive command. When using the no command, give the command once, then repeat it and place the dog on a sit-stay, as a time-out.

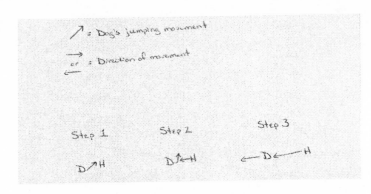

The dog jumps up on the handler. The handler then steps straight into the dog, placing the dog in an insecure position, as the handler comes underneath with one arm brushing both front paws to one side. The handler walks at the dog for a good five to ten feet to make this a negative experience for the dog.

Handler threads his forearm onto the dog's stomach just in front of the dog's hips.

Stay. Come. Heel. Every Time.

*Handler elevates the dog's hind end off the ground
slightly, while taking a giant step away from the
person or object the dog is jumping on.*

Technique Checklist

I have been giving out this Checklist to my clients for
only a couple of years and it has made everyone's lives
much easier. This Checklist should work as a continu-
ous reel in the handler's head. Canines, as mentioned
earlier, are what I call "a total package creature,"
meaning that how you present yourself at all times is
important and that everything has to be checked off if
you expect the dog to do the command at all. This list
does not having any meaning to people who I have not
worked with; however, once the Checklist is learned

from me, through my book or myself, then one will see how simplified a handler's presentation should be. The way I teach is basically in sentence/story format; unfortunately, it is difficult to retrieve your knowledge in the heat of the moment because you do not have the time and patience to go through a story to correct your handling problems. This Checklist is a substitute for "Oh no!" The list covers five positive concept commands and two teaching concepts.

HEEL	SIT	STAY	TAKE-A-BREAK	COME
arm	First:	"sit"	stay	stay
hand	left hand	"stay"	"take-a-break"	attention
leash	right hand	in front		"come"
legs	tug	distance	tug	leash
tugs	"sit"	clock	move away	praise
turns			open arms	"sit"
praise	Second:		praise	
pace	heel			Mistakes:
stops	right hand			jog away
	left hand			opposite side
	angle			tug + release
	"sit"			
				Tips:
				bending down
				open arms

FOLLOW THE LEADER	FREESTYLE
six-foot	twenty-foot
take-a-break	two-thirds
change direction	one-third
tug… "this way"	no heeling
slow walk	
calm praise	
bending down	
head up	
no hints	

This is an explanation of the words on the Checklist to clarify any questions.

HEEL:

> arm = left arm glued to your left side
>
> hand = left hand low on leash and knuckles up, palm down
>
> leash = totally relaxed other than when giving a correction (fraction of a second)
>
> legs = the dog's front legs more/less parallel and even with handler's left leg
>
> tugs = give a tug and release quickly whenever the dog is not in the heel position
>
> turns = sharp U-shaped turns, more left-handed

than right-handed turns

praise = give in between corrections and commands, especially prior to stops

pace = vary walking speed but overall walk
slowly

stops = stop every twenty to forty feet when
things are going well, more often when things
are not

SIT: FIRST

left hand = left hand low on leash

right hand = right hand gives the hand signal

tug = quick tug and release with the left hand on
the leash

"sit" = say sit

SIT: SECOND

heel = handler in the heel position with the dog

right hand = right hand low on leash, where left
hand was previously

left hand = left hand to the dog's left hip so it
cannot scoot away

angle = handler push down on the natural angle
to the dog's back

"sit" = say sit

STAY:

"sit" = say sit and make the dog sit

"stay" = say stay and show the dog the stay hand signal

in front = handler's first step away from the dog is in front of it

distance = handler distances himself or herself slowly

clock = handler walks from three to nine o'clock; dog sits in center of clock

TAKE-A-BREAK:

stay = the dog must be on a sit-stay (the handler must take away the dog's freedom before one can give it to the dog)

"take-a-break" = say take-a-break

tug = give a quick tug and release when saying take-a-break

move away = stepping away entices the dog to follow you

open arms = this is the hand signal to associate with take-a-break

praise = give praise to let the dog know that it is alright to essentially break a stay

COME:

stay = have the dog on a stay; if the dog does not respond from a controlled to a controlled position, then it is not going to work out

attention = get the dog's attention by saying its name and/or praise

"come" = say come and use the hand signal, which is a slap on the thigh

leash = when the dog is on the six-foot leash, you want to reel it in at the same time that the dog is coming in

praise = constantly giving praise from the start to the completion of the command; this is the one time in a dog's life the handler needs the dog to have tunnel (or focused) vision (on the handler)

"sit" = say sit and make the dog sit in front of the handler, within arms reach

Mistakes:

jog away = if the handler tells the dog to come and the dog is walking very slowly, then the handler can jog away to entice the dog to pick up its speed to catch up to the handler

opposite side = if the dog veers off to one side of the beaten path, then the handler takes one giant step in the opposite direction giving the dog a tug and release saying come, once the dog is on the path then the handler takes one giant step back to his/her original position

tug + release = if the handler tells the dog to come and the dog remains on the stay, then the handler should give a quick tug and release and repeat the command

Tips:

bending down = this physical gesture can be very inviting and helpful at times

open arms = this physical gesture can be very inviting and helpful as well the dog will not confuse this with take-a-break

FOLLOW THE LEADER:

six-foot = this concept should be practiced with a six-foot leash

take-a-break = the dog is on a take-a-break at this time

change direction = frequently changing direction forces the dog to pay attention to the handler

tug…"this way" = when the handler changes direction and the dog creates a tense leash by not following, then the handler should give a quick tug and release, saying "this way"

calm praise = giving subdued praise will help to keep the dog calm

slow walk = a slow pace will do the same as calm praise and force the dog to focus on the handler

bending down = when the dog has been doing well, once in awhile the handler should stop and get down on the dog's level to give verbal and physical praise-but only briefly

head up = do not look at the dog during the follow the leader exercise; by not looking at the
dog, the handler can remain focused on what he
or she wants to do

no hints = when changing direction do not say
this way as you make the turn; allow the dog to
figure the concept out on its own

FREESTYLE:

twenty-foot = this exercise is done on the
twenty-foot long leash

two-thirds = the dog is on a take-a-break and
playing

one-third = the dog is on commands given by
the handler

no heeling = the heel command is the one command that is not used in freestyle because it
emphasizes extreme control

Kyle's "The most important thing is…" list

1. First time told, second time fixed.

2. How the *handler handles him- or herself* emotionally and physically.

3. Setting up a good learning environment for
the dog.

4. Knowing the dog's current priorities.

5. Being positive, but assuming the worse—
that way the handler is always prepared for the dog's

mistakes (good behaviors and actions should be the surprises).

6. A dog is only as good as its stay.

7. When in doubt tell the dog to stay.

8. The handler's awareness of the environment has to be at least the equivalent of the dog's awareness of the environment.

9. Once the dog knows the commands, the handler must encourage to discourage the mistakes.

10. Dogs learn in plateaus; allow them some time between having completed one goal and starting the next. This creates a new foundation.

11. Having confidence (not cockiness) is a must.

12. Dogs will never do more than what the handler makes them do.

13. The handler will only get out of a dog what the handler put into the dog.

14. The dog can never handle better than the handler.

15. Patience—dogs do not have deadlines.

16. If the handler is not in control of him- or herself, then the handler will not be in control of the dog. Dog training is all about self-discipline.

17. The dog is evaluating the handler around the clock.

18. Have fun.

19. Evaluate yourself throughout training.

20. The handler always shapes the relationship between them and the dog.

21. Love, trust, and respect.

22. Body language and communication.

23. Do not hesitate.

24. Knowing why dogs do things right and wrong.

25. Knowing the Checklist.

26. The handler should focus on him- or herself and not the dog.

27. Be 50% compassionate and 50% firm, as possible, never the extreme.

28. All progress is through a dog's eyes.

29. Always have high expectations—make the dog impress the handler.

30. Know everything the dog likes and dislikes.

31. *Do not* yell in anger.

32. *Do not* speak passively.

33. *Do* speak assertively with purpose.

34. Create a good physically interactive relationship with the dog.

35. Never have a heavy hand with the dog.

36. Always have a plan for all worst-case scenarios.

37. To experiment (but please think things through first).

38. The highest degree of consistency is absolutely necessary.

39. Realize that this list is only the tip of the iceberg.

Summary of Key Points

🐾 *The building blocks are the basic obedience commands.*

🐾 *Training devices usually include regular flat collar, chain collar (slip collar when placed on correctly), and various length leads from six feet to fifty feet long.*

🐾 *Make the dog earn time off the leash with the commands.*

🐾 **Follow the Leader**: *A take-a-break walk with the dog at either side of the handler or behind the handler, but never in front. Change direction frequently and give a tug if any tension is felt on the lead when the dog does not follow.*

🐾 **Sit**: *When the dog's hind end is on the ground with the front half of the dog's body upright. The hand signal for the sit command is showing the dog the back side of the hand. The sit position is not a natural position that is seen often in nature, so you as the handler have to earn respect prior to complete obedience with this command.*

🐾 **Stay**: *What the basics are all about! A dog is only as good as his or her stay. This command is always a* sit-stay when a dog is allowed to lay down, sit back up, and spin three hundred sixty degrees, as long as the dog's hind end remains exactly where the handler placed it. The hand signal for the stay command is showing the dog the palm of the hand. The stay establishes physical control and encourages maximum mental motion. The three mental stages of the stay are the alert, absorbing, and relaxed stages.

Come: The dog has to go from a distant point to a controlled sit position, in front of the handler within arm's reach. The hand signal for the come command is a slap on the thigh. This command is taught from a stay position. Giving constant praise is one of the most crucial factors in getting the dog to appropriately execute the come command. When calling the dog with the come command, the handler should bend down as the dog responds. Do not approach the canine if it slows down—this becomes less inviting.

Down: All four paws and legs are flat out on the ground. Depending upon the environment, a dog might view the down position as a bad position. Teach the down by saying "down" when the dog lays down on his or her own. Canine Instinct does not employ the down command as part of its basic obedience in today's programs.

Heel: The dog is "at left." This command requires time and self-discipline to develop the coordination and confidence to execute this command. Think of the heel as a "mental race." The handler gives the dog a task at the rate at which it can think. The handler maintains the dog's attention with frequent turns, variation of pace, and stops. The heel command is second in the line of importance (second only to the stay command). This command shows a dog that the handler is able to give it guidance on the *go—it is a very impressive command.*

🦅 **Take-a-Break**: *The dog may do whatever he or she wants within reason. The hand signal is showing the dog wide open arms. This command is taught from a stay position.*

🦅 **Freestyle**: *Play time with rules. Two-thirds play and one-third work time use all the basic commands except for the heel command. The handler should make sure that the dog is constantly engaged in his or her activity. The stays will be short due to play/work ratio.*

🦅 **Boundary Training**: *A "contextual stay" concept. The dog does not have to sit with this correction, just remain inside the permitted area. Introduce the correction from the outside to the inside, then later switch to starting from the inside to the outside. Try to use physically delineating boundaries to make the boundary clearer. Shout "stay" when the dog steps on or across the line. Scurry or walk the dog five to ten feet back inside the line after a mistake, then go right back to the broken area.*

🦅 **No**: *The negative concept command that is used in jumping, barking, biting, mouthing, and destructive situations. Do not use the "no" command when executing any positive concept command situations. The handler can bring a positive idea to a negative situation but not a negative idea to a positive situation. The handler needs to encourage the problem to discourage the problem. "Flooding" is frequently used, but in small doses. The element of surprise is very helpful in getting the dog to care about his or her wrongful behaviors.*

Additional Basic Obedience
And Concepts

Helpful Commands

These commands can be applied to a dog's daily routine: **give, leave it, inside, out, spot, kennel up, over, and back.** Having the leash on your dog for teaching these commands is helpful. Certainly you can have the leash off when you know the dog will comply. When dealing with positional commands, it is good to point to where you want the dog to go—a physical gesture goes a long way with a dog. Just a reminder: *First time told, second time fixed* is in effect.

Give

Give is used when a handler wants to take an object from the dog. When the handler says "give," the dog should open its mouth so the handler can take the object without any resistance. To teach a dog to give involves either one of two or both methods of mine.

Regardless of which way it is done, it is best to place the dog on a sit-stay to get the dog thinking about the handler. The one method that I traditionally use is *the blowing in the ear technique*; this is an old hunting dog trick. The handler says "give" once. After a second, if the dog is refusing to give, the handler should blow into the dog's ear in a fairly strong manner, with one hand on the object. When you blow in its ear, the dog will let go of the object and look at you thinking, "Hey, stop it!" Immediately after the blow in the ear, the handler should stand up with the object, and say "give" at the same time.

The alternative method can be a bit more firm. I usually will take away all the dog's toys except the rope toys. I will use the rope toy to play with the dog and then tell the dog to sit...stay...give. If the dog does not give, I hold the rope toy with both hands while it is in the dog's mouth, push the rope toy back at the dog, and then quickly pull it back toward myself, out of the dog's mouth. If neither method works, that usually means it is being done incorrectly or the dog has some aggression issues, in which case the toy should not be taken out. Regardless of what anyone says, if the dog is aggressive there is no benefit in taking it out of its mouth. Aggression issues mean that the handler has to get inside the dog's head, not his or her mouth! These methods are obviously not recommended for any dog that has known aggression issues. For this kind of dog, I will use the follow the leader technique to get the dog to drop the toy. This is a last resort, because if the dog is forced to think about the handler, then it will drop the toy. The handler must change direction a lot to get this to work.

Tell the dog to give the object being held; if the dog refuses, then pick up the dog's ear and give a good firm blow.

Leave It

This command is easy to teach. *Leave it* means drop the item because it cannot come into the house. When the two of you reach the door any time the dog wants bring a stick into the house or car, say "leave it" and the dog should drop it. If after a second he or she does not drop it, then remove it from his or her mouth and leave it outside. Sometimes people use this command when they should be using the no command. Be careful; if you can benefit from this command, then just make sure that you use it. In about a month's time, the dog will fully understand. You probably will not have to use it too often after that because the dog will know that certain things just cannot come into the house or car.

Inside and Out

Inside means to go inside the house and *out* means to go outside of the house. Again, just make sure that when you go in and out and the dog goes with you and that you say "inside" or "out," whichever one is appropriate. In a month's time the dog will have this down with no problem.

Kennel Up

Kennel up means to go into an enclosure, either a car or a kennel. Whenever you want the dog to go into the car or kennel, he or she should say "kennel up." Place the dog in the car or kennel in the event that the animal does not cooperate or is not paying attention. If the dog tends to resist, I would recommend having the leash on the dog.

Some dogs, especially larger ones, will balk at jumping into a vehicle. Opening all the doors and in a positive but assertive fashion go in one side of the car and out the other side. This makes the dog feel like he's not trapped.

Over and Back

For those of you who do not mind where your dog is in the car, these two commands are useful. *Over* means to go from the driver's seat to the passenger seat. The handler says "Over" to get the dog to do this. *Back* means to go from the front seat of the car to the back seat of the car. The handler says "Back" to get the dog to do this. If you want the dog to remain in the back seat, place the dog on a sit-stay. If the dog resists, the leash could be of help with this command.

Spot

This command is absolutely great for the family dog. *Spot* means to go to the area that the handler has designated as the dog's spot and remain there until otherwise told. Spot should be taught with a leash on to make things more upbeat and easy. The handler should gradually wean the dog off the leash as he or she becomes more consistent with responding to the spot command. The location of the spot will vary depending upon the house setup. It should be in a place away from the entrance of the house, but in which the dog can clearly see the entrance. This allows the family to greet guests without the dog being in the way.

I often teach this in relation to a knock at the door or the doorbell ringing, so that eventually the dog will go to its spot when he or she hears a knock or ring. However, to make this a *positive* command, I initially use and teach it as a separate concept from someone being at the door. The handler says "spot" and walks the dog to the spot location, pointing and bending low as the handler places him or her on a sit-stay followed by lots of praise. Praise should be given all the way to the spot. It is nice to be able to have the spot where the dog can lie down while it is your family's meal time too, but if the house's structure does not allow for the spot to serve a duel purpose, then simply use a sit-stay or come up with another word for another spot. Spot should definitely be used for visitors at the door, so make sure to choose a location that is appropriate. You want the dog to view the spot command in a positive light. For this to happen, use this command as much as possible at other times besides the whole door-greeting scenario. This will make the dog feel good rather than bad when the greeting occurs; the dog will not feel like he or she is being restrained from someone he or she very much wants to see. Twenty-five percent of the time the spot command will be used when greetings occur (use the spot 100% of the time someone arrives). Try to balance using the spot command in more positively viewed scenarios around 75% of the time. See pictures for assistance.

The handler is walking from where the dog wants to be over to the spot location saying "spot" as soon as they start to walk. The handler points to the spot the whole way there.

*The handler stands up and talks to the dog
when arriving at the spot location, then distances
himself away from the dog.*

Summary of Key Points

❧ **Give**: To hand over the object that the dog is carrying in his or her mouth. The correction is followed by a blow in the ear. Do not do this with nasty dogs, as they will bite the handler. The push and pull method for corrective purposes is another option.

❧ **Leave It**: To not touch or drop it where the dog is at because the handler does not want the dog to have contact with the object at that time.

❧ **Inside and Out**: Useful when teaching housebreaking.

Kennel Up: A way to overcome resistance when it is time for the dog to go in the kennel before work, bed, or travel.

Over and Back: To get the dog out of the way in relationship to where the handler is at.

All these concepts are very easily incorporated into daily routine. These concepts are all that is needed for success.

Children With Canines

Working with Children

This is a topic that must be clearly understood for both child and dog. Proper training of children around dogs is crucial. A parent/handler must realize that both the child and the dog can be totally innocent yet both can get seriously hurt. It is the parent/handler's responsibility to make sure that the dog is raised and educated well to minimize and prevent all unhealthy avenues of canine behavior. Educating and managing children with dogs is equally or perhaps more important. In my opinion, *management* is the parent/handler's number one priority. This will keep the child safe. Educating a young child about anything can be difficult. In terms of safety, a six-year-old child's retention of any cautions cannot be relied upon.

I introduce children into my training program usually about halfway through. This way the parent and I have gained progress with the dog before working together with the child and the dog. Any rules that apply to the parent, apply to the child as well. We make the child's task simpler. I have the child work with sit, stay, come, and take-a-break to start. All of the child's work is done with me or the parent physically assisting him or her as the child attempts the commands. As the child's understanding progresses, and the dog gets better with the child, we work with the heel command as well. It depends upon the dog, but many times I am hesitant to have the child use the negative concept commands in case the dog becomes aggressive—of course, this depends upon the individual dog.

The system that I use with children, which has worked well for me, is my *Canine Kid Superstar Program*. Children find this fun. I and/or parents reward children according to how well they were listening to us and following our rules during the week. Their reward or motivation can be an ice cream cone, an extra half hour of television, a small toy, or preferably, a new dog trick to do with their dog, whatever it takes to have the child retain what has been taught to them. At the end of the session I ask them questions and the children are rewarded if they answer correctly. I also give the child a report card grade based on attentiveness. Many children try harder with their dog when a score is given out (adults too).

Aggression Awareness

I also want to stress to dog owners who are also parents is that teaching your child to be safe around dogs that display aggressive behaviors is of paramount importance. First, children and known aggressive dogs are not to be trusted around one another. But an unexpected attack from your trusted family dog can happen, too. If a dog goes to bite a child, I teach the child to immediately turn from the dog and take two to three steps away; at the same time the child should cover his or her face with the hands and yell for mom or dad. I do not want the child to run away from the dog because if the dog is nasty and/or crazed, then it might chase the child. Taking those two or three steps away will not entice the dog to run after the child, and if the dog is going to just snap once for whatever reason, hopefully the child will be fast enough to take that step away from the dog that has no intention of following the child. Additionally, if there is a wall nearby, then I recommend the child turn and face the wall to maximally protect his or her body. If no wall is near, then the child should cover the face with his or her hands. This is probably good to do anyway.

To avoid any confrontations between a child and a dog, I tell children *never* to take a toy, treat, bone, or any other object from a dog without the consent and supervision of his or her parent. You should be able to take anything away from any dog, but should be able to and actually being able to are two different things. Guessing the outcome is not worth the risk! The parent and I will drill the dog in this area; our practice is as real as I can make it, depending upon the dog being worked. Teaching children how to properly physically interact with a canine can be incredibly challenging too. No tail pulling, no ear pulling, no horseback rides, no screaming, and no fast or unusual movements around a dog are things to be reinforced to the child again and again. Of course, children do just about all of these things naturally.

As a parent, teach your children as I am teaching you, on a level they can understand that will sink in and stick! Prevention through education is the best protection you and I have to offer children.

Summary of Key Points

🐾 *Parents have to assume responsibilities for their children around dogs.*

🐾 *Have the dog doing well for the parent prior to the child handling the dog.*

🐾 *Once children are introduced into training, all the rules apply to them too—just simplify the tasks.*

🐾 *The Canine Kid Superstar Program: bribe the children for their "attention," then they will learn.*

🐾 *Lay ground rules with the child; never take anything away from a dog, be physically gentle, speak calmly (normal), and try not to be so animated.*

🐾 *Constant supervision with children and dogs is strongly recommended.*

🐾 *Teach children to cover their face and turn to face a wall or nearby object when a dog is jumping or being aggressive with them.*

🐾 *Prevention through education!*

Pals With Problems

Defining the Problem and Getting Started

These canines are always a challenge! About a third or so of the dogs I have worked with fit into this category. Many forms of aggression, destructiveness, barking, and separation anxiety are issues that these four-legged friends have displayed. All of these problems are associated with the negative concept command "no," when applicable. When dealing with aggression, you must first identify the undesirable behavior as either acquired or neurotic. *Acquired* meaning a learned behavior that is voluntary. *Neurotic* meaning an innate and involuntary action. Once the behavior is recognized as one or the other, you can then determine our approach. If acquired, then you use techniques to fix the problem, whereas, if neurotic, you minimize and manage the problem.

It is a big responsibility to make sure that all canines are safe, or can be made to be safe, in a household and community. These groups of dogs that we are talking about are dogs that most people neglect and avoid dealing with their problems. *Please make an attempt* to see what can be done to help the situation or remove the unfit canine from your home. Finding someone who can and is willing to help an individual with a dog that has aggression problems can be difficult.

To mention some important points about working with these kinds of dogs briefly: first, do not make any eye contact with a canine that is displaying any aggression. If you look into a dog's eyes, you will either provoke the dog to become defensive or offensive, neither of which is good. There is zero benefit in making eye contact in this situation. The physical and vocal gestures of the dog should be more than enough to make a handler aware of the frame of mind of a canine. Second, *no heavy-handed techniques are to be used!* The more aggressive the handler gets, more times than not the canine gets more aggressive too. Even if the canine's negative behavior comes to a halt, the dog often becomes fearful and/or aloof. Third, if able, I always prefer to have a month or two of basic obedience under my belt with an aggressive dog prior to bringing out a dog's worst state. Once the canine respects the handler and has an education to fall back on, it makes a world of difference in your progress with an aggressive canine. Destructiveness, barking, and separation anxiety often have a lower success rate in correcting than aggression; however, I have had good results on a whole with my methods. Despite lack of complete success in these areas, there are management techniques that work well.

Aggression

Aggression is dangerous to work with. Only individuals who have been taught well or naturally understand where the canine is coming from with its aggression should attempt to correct these behaviors. **I do not recommend that a handler work with these dogs, unless all risks and responsibilities are understood by the handler.** Everything mentioned in this section is a rough outline of what I do. I have worked with over three hundred dogs with serious problems of varying degrees. Every canine must be approached cautiously, yet with confidence. A handler must have a plan for the eventuality of any conceivable canine attack, prior to entering the fire.

Once I am so close to a dog that if it goes to bite me I could not back away fast enough, then I go straight toward the dog. Canines do not expect nor do they like surprises. When a dog comes at a person to bite, it usually does not expect that person to move toward it. If I feel that I can benefit from the leash being on for a correction, then I will use it. When a dog comes at me and I move toward it, my usual plan is to go directly toward its head and either run into the dog, or push its neck away as I stand up, or push the dog's body around to pick up its rear end by threading an arm between the front and rear legs, raising the rear end with my forearm on the dog's stomach. Once the dog's back end is off the ground, it makes it difficult for the dog to attack. If the dog goes for me again, I throw its hind end right at the dog's head. I call this my *forearm technique*. I then remove the dog from its target (including myself). If I am able, I follow up with a firm sit-stay (a long one). Try to stand up as soon as possible because your standing height is a major advantage.

If you are a few feet or more away from the dog when it goes to bite, stand straight up and use your feet to ward off the dog. Do not retreat! Stand tall, looking in the direction of the canine but make *no eye* contact. Firmly, say "no...sit...stay." If possible, do not yell. This emphasizes a lack of control on the handler's behalf, and that is never good with an aggressive canine that already feels the handler is not in control. Depending on the dog and the situation, I will use a large towel or a small bed sheet to throw over the canine while it is attacking its target. First, to prevent the dog from biting, and second, to be able to physically correct the canine more safely.

To minimize aggressive behavior when working with an aggressive canine, I recommend slow movements and patience. Try not to force a dog to make progress too quickly. I have described several things that I do during an aggressive attack. Knowing what to do and actually performing the proper corrections at the optimum time are often the two things that a novice handler or a handler who lacks confidence has trouble with. One needs to have quick responses when in the fire. It is do or get bitten! You can miserably fail in handling a dog then quickly recover to make the mistake seem like the failure never happened. Aggressive canines are serious and they mean business. If you are a handler who could potentially have a brain freeze or resort to *typical* human responses, then you are fried. If a handler cannot "walk the walk," then he or she should not try to get inside this kind of canine's head.

These are the areas of canine aggression that I deal with most often: food, toy, canine, people, and other animal aggression. Often we see dogs that have several of these problems.

I do want to mention that I often wear leather gloves, boots, chaps, and sometimes even a thick but flexible jacket when I work with these kinds of dogs.

There are no key point summaries at the end of these sections because every tiny detail counts with these dogs—all dogs—but especially these dogs.

Food Aggression

Food aggression is a situation that, if fixable, will usually take me up to three months to resolve. Food aggression often develops because there is no human present often enough during the dog's daily feeding routine. The canine views his or her food as something that it has complete control over, and displays this control with aggressive actions and/or gestures. During the first two to three weeks of dealing with such a problem, I divide the dog's daily rations into thirds or preferably quarters. Regardless of the owner's work schedule, the dog must be fed at least three times per day. By increasing the frequency of meals, the problem can be corrected more quickly. I give the dog approximately ten minutes to eat each portion. There are several stages to the process; I strongly recommend doing all of these stages with the leash in case it is needed.

During the first phase I only feed the canine out of my hand. This is not to make the canine dependent upon me, but rather to make the canine feel it is eating *with* me, a positive concept. In phase one, the first two to three weeks, the food bowl is put away out of sight. This is to break the custom or expected routine that had encouraged the aggressive behavior. I will also use a new bowl to help reduce the dog's possessiveness of the bowl. During and after this training, the dog should be fed in a different room than previously. The handler at this stage should speak words of praise when the dog is nonaggressive in situations where it would have usually been aggressive.

As mentioned, the dog eats strictly from the handler's hand during this phase. The other hand should be gently stroking the canine to desensitize him or her. I prefer to be *squatting on the side* of the dog, holding the bowl in hand with the food in front of the dog at his or her eye level. I specifically squat and *do not sit*, so I can quickly move if need be. I am on the *side* so the canine cannot get a straight shot at its target (me!). If the dog becomes aggressive, I would push the dog as far away from me as possible, as I stand up to a safer level. When squatting, I try to be as close to the dog's *side* as possible so the dog has difficulty if he or she tries to quickly bite me. As I stand up, I give a firm no...sit...stay. If the dog starts to growl, I never say, "no," even if I am in a remotely vulnerable position.

This is because I do not want to ignite a fire prematurely and put myself at risk of injury.

If the canine has an aggressive moment, then the correction is given and the exercise is over. The next attempt will be at the next meal. Do not add the canine's leftovers from his or her previous meal. This also goes for when he or she does not finish his or her food in ten minutes. If it takes longer then three weeks to accomplish the objective, then I keep with the program. Regardless of how well the dog might be doing, even if the dog has never once made a groan, I still do phase one for a solid two weeks. Upon *successful completion* of phase one, we move on to phase two.

My physical position, the number of meals, the lengths of meals, and the correction of the canine are the same as in phase one. In this phase, I hold the food bowl (an entirely new food bowl) at the canine's eye level while the canine eats. Stroke the dog as in the earlier phase. This phase takes a minimum of two weeks.

In phase three, the physical position, the number of weeks (providing expected results are occurring), and the correction of the canine are the same as during the previous two phases. In this stage, food is placed in the new bowl, the handler places one of his or her hands on top of that, and more food is placed on top of the handler's hand. The bowl is on the floor. The other hand still strokes the canine softly and words of praise are given. Certainly in this phase when and if the opportunity to increase the frequency of feeding times it can help a lot. Also go through the first half of the process but with no food in the bowl, as this can help take off the edge by making the bowl not as important. Another thing to do to take the edge off is to put the dog on a sit-stay for a few minutes prior to approaching the bowl with the dog. This calms the dog down prior to going into the *fire*. Remember to have the leash on when doing this exercise. Phase three should be done for a minimum of two weeks.

Phase four is the phase when the stakes are raised. Again, everything that has been done in the previous phases is still in effect. In this phase, I put food in the bowl (no hands in the bowl) and gently stroke the *same side* of the dog that I am on. This is because if the dog attacks me, I can use both hands to push the dog away as I stand up. Depending on where the handler is, he or she can use my forearm technique. This is often the first major problem phase. The canine could possibly view this as the old way of eating his or her meals. The goal with the first three phases is to have the canine reassess its environment and priorities, hopefully noticing the situation is not serious or threatening. The fourth phase should be in effect for a minimum of three weeks.

Phase five, the final stage, involves the handler placing the food bowl on the floor with food in it and then distancing himself or herself from the dog, still squatting at the dog's side but now several feet away. I work my way away from the dog and back in toward the dog. When getting close to the dog, I give the dog a few strokes on his or her side. If the dog goes to make a bad move or vocalization, then I will grab the leash and pull the dog away from the food, while telling it no…sit…stay firmly, making the canine do it. Once I have worked this phase successfully for at least two weeks, then a good part of the food aggression problem has been resolved. At this time if I feel comfortable without the leash then I can take it off the dog.

Do realize that the handlers of the canine benefit the most from this method as well as any children who might be around the aggressive dog during its meal times. The handler must be aware of the potential danger of a food-aggressive dog. I have seen dogs that revert to an instinctive but insane primal state over food. Remember that food is needed to survive and some canines might have difficulty with the remote possibility of having to give up their food. The insanity switch goes on and there is no reasoning with the dog in that state of mind. Progress with these dogs often will be slower then desired. When working with these problem areas, please make sure to go slowly. Do not attempt to rush the dog into the next phase until the current phase has been completed with consistent success. **I recommend getting hands-on professional help with this problem due to the potential risks.**

Toy Aggression

Toy trouble is another common problem with dogs. Dogs can get very possessive with their toys. Practice as much as possible to correct this problem. Many canines have issues with toys because they are naturally very greedy animals. If a dog takes this point of view, you must know how to deal with this outwardly greedy individual. As a reminder, I advise the leash be on just in case.

In phase one, the handler holds the toy and strokes the dog, allowing the dog to play with the toy. The positioning of the handler in this phase is in a squat at the dog's *side*. If the canine displays any undesirable behavior, the handler pushes the canine away while standing up, saying, "no...sit...stay." The sit-stay is used as a time-out for the dog's poor decision making, as in the food aggression section. During this phase, there should not be any toys around the house. The only time the canine gets to play with the toy is when the handler holds it. Phase one should be done for at least one week or until satisfactory results are achieved.

Phase two is the same as phase one, except that if the canine behaves well, his or her reward is to get to play with the toy all by itself. When the dog stops playing with the toy, for whatever reason, take the toy away. Wait until the dog leaves the toy by itself before removing it. By doing this you are instilling only positive interaction with the dog in relation to toys. While in phase two, I frequently practice phase one. Phase two should be continued for at least one week or until satisfactory results occur.

Phase three is the final phase. I like to have a small box where all the toys are stored. I often use a cat litter pan and put it some place out of the way. I teach the dog that this is *my* box, with *my* toys, and the dog can only go into it and use *my* toys when I say he or she can. I continue the use of the toy box throughout the canine's life. During the last phase, the practice of the first two phases should be continued. Take a toy and place it on the floor of a room, then enter the room with the dog on a leash. Walk the dog up to the toy and have the dog take it. Tell the dog to sit-stay prior to removing the toy from the dog's mouth, by giving the give command. This sit-stay places the dog under control and hopefully makes the dog more conscious of your innocent action. If the canine gets aggressive, then say "no" and move the dog to a new nearby location and repeat the sit-stay. If the handler has trouble with doing another sit-stay, then try doing a very fast follow the leader, pacing back and forth; since dogs can think only one thing at a time, the dog will often drop the object in its mouth. The handler can then place the dog on a sit-stay and pick up the toy.

An alternative approach is to walk into the room and place the dog on a sit-stay, then pick up the toy and give it to the dog, but never let go of it. Follow this by tossing the toy a few feet in front of the dog and then having the dog pick it up. Give lots of praise at this time and try to get the canine as happy as possible. This is a form of desensitization that can make the toy less important to the dog in the long run. The leash should still be on while working your way close to the dog and grabbing the base of the leash, near the dog's head. While the dog is on this take-a-break, nicely and firmly grab the toy in a playful sense and take it away. Again, remember how to counteract an aggressive attack from the dog as discussed in phase one. If you feel comfortable, then remove the leash at this point. The last phase can take a while to work successfully.

Continuing the other two phases throughout greatly helps. The average turn-around time with toy issues is normally about one to two months. **Again, I recommend getting professional hands-on help with this problem due to the potential risks.**

Canine Aggression

This kind of aggression involves a little more of an adrenaline rush. Controlling one canine is difficult enough. Occasionally the workload doubles because the other dog retaliates, but often the aggressor is still the main focal point. I have had very good luck with my methods in all canine aggressive problems mentioned in this section, but canine aggression has always had the best results. Depending upon the case, however, it can take the longest to accomplish. I am always very optimistic with the vast majority of these types of aggression problems. There are basically three situations that commonly occur: one canine attacks and the other submits; one canine attacks and the other attacks as well; or a canine wants to attack, but physically cannot reach the other canine. Aggressive canines can fit into one or all three of these categories. As stated in all other aggression training, I strongly recommend the leash and the supervision of an experienced professional.

When a canine attacks another canine, the fur flies as they say. First let's get one thing clear: I *never* put my hands between the two dogs in the midst of battle! This is pure stupidity! Let's break down this aggressive scenario step by step: you have an advantage in correcting this aggressive problem, because you are not the primary target. This usually allows you to physically correct the dog using my forearm technique. With dogs that have a higher risk of turning around to bite you, throw a blanket or bedsheet over the dog prior to using my forearm technique. The sheet serves as protection from the canine that you are correcting. Obviously, the sheet is only available in situations where we set up the dog. As the correction is given, make sure to say a firm "no." Once you have separated the dogs from one another, the aggressor should be placed on a sit-stay. This is used as a time-out. This stay should be a few minutes or so.

When setting up a situation, also have the leash on the dog until the dog starts to improve his or her behavior. I use the dog that is most commonly attacked, or if not possible, then a trained dog that is responsive to me, as bait. Using a dog that is often exposed to the aggressive dog often will trigger the behavior we are trying to discourage. I try to use a dog that does not retaliate. Using a trained dog helps in controlling the aggressor and lowers the risks of the overall situation at hand. The reason that I must encourage this undesired behavior is so that we can discourage it. I do not have to try to do this secretly. I actually want the dog to know that I am setting it up. Due to my previous correction(s), the canine already knows that the targeted behavior is wrong, so now when I go to encourage the behavior, the dog often starts thinking about the situation on a deeper level. I want the aggressive dog to get sick of the handler correcting its aggressive behavior and get the message. Out of the three possible aggressive canine situations, this problem is the best one to deal with from a handler's point of view.

Another problem that can get very nasty is when one canine attacks and the other canine retaliates. This is very dangerous! If the fights are serious, my number one recommendation is to remove one of the dogs from the household, because the owner has certainly bitten off more than he or she can chew. Obedience must be enforced and executed well with both dogs before introducing them *together* into an environment and atmosphere where they are likely to snap at one another. The correction used with this problem is the same as in our first area of discussion. My forearm technique is preferred in this case. Also, when both canines attack each other, I still will only use one leash. I do not want to risk getting the two dogs tangled up together so that I cannot separate them. I use my own judgment as to how I feel about which dog would benefit more from wearing the leash, if either. To ideally correct the canines in this situation, I like to have another handler, one handler for each dog. This way, while correcting one, the other does not continue to attack. Handlers often get bitten when attempting to handle such a situation alone. It is best to stomp out *both fires* at the same time. This is much easier said than done! I place myself at the most risk with this kind of aggressive issue.

I usually correct the dog that initiated the aggressive

behavior. This canine is purely on the offensive, so usually grabbing this one tends to be safer for the handler. When there are two handlers, use two leashes. I have the second handler correct the other canine. If the leash is used at all, I have found it to be most useful if and when the aggressor is corrected and the other dog lunges for the now vulnerable dog. In this case, if the handler is not fast enough to use his or her forearm, then the leash is available. This is generally my approach to this problem.

The last common canine aggression problem that I often deal with is when one dog is waiting to viciously attack a dog that it cannot get to. Whether the situation is an aggressive dog in the house, looking out the window, in the car, or walking on the road with the owner, all these are regular phone calls that I receive regarding this problem area. I will explain what I do in each situation.

When a dog is displaying aggressive behavior in the house, looking out the window, the no command is first used; if the dog does not respond, then the second time say, "no...sit...stay." Make sure to place the canine away from its vantage point. When setting up the canine in this situation, I like to start off with the leash on so I can pull the dog away from the window while telling the dog, "no...sit...stay." I keep a cup of water handy to wet my hand and flick my fingers at the dog to get its attention with a spritz of water in its' face. If little progress is made with this technique, then I rearrange the room, so that the dog cannot look out the window. This will break up the undesirable routine a bit. Keep the room arrangement different for two weeks or so before going back to the old arrangement and trying again. On the other hand, if the new arrangement looks nice, let's stick with that!

It can be difficult to control the situation when the dog is displaying aggressive behavior in the car. Practicing the sit-stay in the car at home, in the driveway, with the car not running is a start. Place the dog on a sit-stay behind the passenger seat with the leash on. This way if there is only one person in the car then the driver has the dog in the best position for correction. Place the leash between the two front seats, onto the driver /handler's lap. Start off by just sitting in the car with the dog for a good five minutes or more. After that goes well, get in and out of the car and walk around the car. This whole time continue to make sure that the dog is on a sit-stay behind the passenger seat. Once consistently good results are achieved, then sit in the car and start it up. Turn on the radio, the direction-als/flashers, put the windows down and up, honk the horn—all of these can trigger a dog to break the stay. With this we are working our way to desensitizing the dog to everything but the main event. Next the han-dler should drive up and down the driveway, then a road that is not too busy, lastly through a town or village. If the dog gets up at any time, then the handler should start correcting the dog by saying "sit-stay," using the hand signal, and giving just a quick tug and release forward to get the dog's attention. If there is any aggressive behavior, then the handler should do the exact same thing and say "no...sit...stay." Please be careful—remember you are still driving. If you are able to stop the car or pull over to correct the dog, then please do.

When walking the dog on the road, the handler should always walk on the left side of the road or the right side if the main distraction is also on the left side. There are several techniques to try. First I will heavily drill the dog with heeling and follow the leader once I see an approaching distraction to get the most control of the dog as possible. When the distraction is passing by, I will continue to walk with the dog in a heel. If the dog gets aggressive, I continue to walk without stopping and continue to give corrections, saying "no," because of the aggressive behavior being displayed. If there is no aggressive behavior displayed, only extreme interest in the distraction, then do the same exact thing except say "heel" instead of no. If progress does not seem to occur, then I would make the dog do a sit-stay as the distraction approaches rather than heel the dog on by. With aggressive dogs I prefer to heel the dog on by the distraction because this does not allow the dog to become completely fixated on the distraction, whereas on a stay the dog is absorbing sometimes to the point of indulgence. But if the heeling does not work, then the stay will. **I advise you to seek professional hands-on assistance with these problems.**

Aggressive Canine Conclusion

With the forms of aggression touched upon, I cannot tell you how long it will take for resolution. Do make

sure when working with these dogs that before jumping into the fire you make sure that you have some
respect from them or else I feel that your efforts will be
nearly pointless. Make sure that the "stays" used for
time-outs are fairly long. Keep your head high and
stick to the plan. The hardest thing about aggressive
situations is being able to have a clear head in the
thick of it. Handlers can apply the negative concept
command and the aggression training strategy to situations where dogs have problems with people and other
animals. **Remember what I said in the beginning of
this section: I do not recommend that you work with
these dogs without a trainer or without extensive
experience. Always remember that there is never
a guarantee when dealing with these kinds of
behaviors.**

Destructiveness

Destructiveness can often be prevented and solved
using the crate, which is explained in detail in the
third chapter. Destruction issues that deal with situations other than the owner being away from home can
often be worked out. When using the no command,
make sure to follow the rules closely. A common
problem is the chewing of clothing and shoes. When
dealing with the negative concept command, flood the
dog so he or she views the problem as a problem, just
as what has been done in all other negative training
situations. Throw clothing, shoes, tissues, whatever it
might be that the dog likes to destroy, on the floor.

Also put the dog's toys on the floor so when the dog goes to pick up the toys you can give praise to help differentiate between good and bad. Then actively play with the dog to get it into the frame of mind in which it is most likely not to listen! Playing should encourage the canine to act poorly and take the bait. *Encourage the problem to discourage the problem.* When the dog goes to pick up something that it should not, you should immediately say "no...sit...stay." The stay should last for a minute or so. You should continue to do this until the dog understands and no longer wants to participate anymore. Try this method first. If it does not work, then try spraying Bitter Apple (specific brand of spray deterrent) on the objects desired by the dog. You should have success with either one or a combination of these methods to stop destructive behavior (along with proper crate training).

Set up this situation everyday, multiple times per day. Let the canine know you are setting it up. There is no secret here. You really need to have the mentality: "Here is the problem. This is how we fix it, and do it until it doesn't happen anymore." This concept certainly applies for aggression as well as for barking. With destructive behavior, you can place the dog in a crate if the dog is destructive when you are not home. Seldom will a dog continue to misbehave in front of you after going through these motions. If a dog does, then having him or her on a stay in your presence ensures that a dog will not be destructive.

Barking

Barking can be extremely difficult to stop. The no...sit...stay is still enforced here. This emphasizes that *one must have control of the dog physically prior to having control vocally.* Once the handler is on the dog's mind, then the dog is likely to remain silent or at least have the no command mean more. When correcting the canine for barking, the only thing that I might do in addition to what was previously mentioned is to keep a water dish handy. I wet my fingers and flick them at the dog while saying "no." Many dogs do not like this trick. I prefer not to use a squirt bottle because the canine learns the handler's limitations. I would say that roughly seventy-five percent of the time I have resolved barking problems. If there is not much success with this strategy, then to help manage the problem I will turn on the radio or television on low volume to muffle any noise that might encourage the dog to bark. This has had a decent success rate considering the significance of the problem.

Separation Anxiety

Destructiveness and barking often occur due to separation anxiety. I have had the most difficult time solving this problem in an ideal fashion. I have only recommended medication for dogs five times in my life for behavioral problems, and three out five were for dogs with seriously severe separation anxiety. Separation anxiety can occur for many reasons: neurosis, neglect, past abuse—or simply because the dog lives too much of the good life! Nowadays many people work at home, and people are around their dogs all the time; to be separated from the owner for any length of time causes complete hysteria within a dog's head. This, of course, depends on the individual dog's personality. Often, having a routine where the owner is away from the dog for a certain length of time from puppyhood or from adoption is best. The alternative is to always have someone around the dog to nullify any undesired behaviors due to the owner's absence. When dealing with barking and destructiveness caused by separation anxiety, follow directions as previously instructed. Canines that have this problem are often insecure with themselves and the environment they are in. Sometimes the more "stays" a canine does a distance away from the handler (as in not touching the handler), the more the canine not only learns and accepts its environment but also develops a level of independence (due to physically being separated from the owner), allowing the dog to think more freely.

Pals with Problems Conclusion

All of these problems are interconnected because, when applicable, you can use the corrections for one issue to help solve another and because, remember, all problems are due to a lack of education and respect. People who have canines with the issues that I have touched upon in this section have a heavy workload, if they want to make things work out. Make the dog as educated and respectful as possible; if needed, attempt the strategies mentioned here according to the problem at hand.

Live, Laugh, And Learn: Canine Stories

These short anecdotes are all true stories about some of my experiences in past years. I wanted to share a few of them with you regarding the wonderful world of dogs: their abilities, their intelligence, and their overall potential. I have included stories from a few different areas of my work with the canine to give you a well-rounded perspective. I hope you enjoy these stories; laugh at some, and learn from all that I have shared.

Basic Obedience: Napping or Not?

Several years back, I taught two golden retrievers in the same household at the same time. These dogs were littermates, a brother and sister. They were both wonderful family companions that did well with their basic obedience program. These goldens were dogs that really tune into what the handler is doing. Perhaps too tuned in....

I started to work with these dogs during the summer months and that July was brutally hot! Well, frequently, on hot summer days, I work dogs in short segments, and then place them in the shade on a stay. The dogs usually lie down and go to sleep, which is fine with me. When the dog wakes up, I normally relieve them of their duties. I allow this because I certainly do not remember the last thing that I was thinking about when I fall asleep!

Well, I started to realize that these two dogs' naps were getting shorter and shorter as the weather got hotter and hotter. These golden retrievers had realized that they were on a take-a-break when they awoke from the nap they took after I put them on a stay! It became apparent that every time I placed them on a sit-stay they would lay down, close their eyes, then immediately get up and walk around! So I had to tell them to stay when they woke up from their pretend naps. What started off innocently over time had developed into a *purposely wrongful action*, once these golden retrievers became aware of my lenience. Canines will never do more than what one makes them do, especially when dealing with things that are not particularly fun. Do not let innocent mistakes turn into big problems down the road. If innocent mistakes are being consistently made, then certainly fix them!

Aggressive Behavior: Think Before You Bite!

I have taught many aggressive canines in my life and in a noteworthy percentage I never get to see the aggression because of the respect that I develop in the dog, and because of the quality of communication that I strive for in relating to the dog. Before I feed an aggressive dog to the fire (its' troublesome area), I gain respect by teaching the basic commands necessary to control the dog in its aggressive state. Once I introduce a dog to the fire, a dog will often not act the way it has been acting for the owner. This is good because the problem is respect but also bad because it requires a lot of work for the owner to gain respect. One has to be willing to put forth the effort to gain the respect.

I taught two German shepherds that loved one another *to pieces*. The only problem was that the older one, a female, had taken the younger one, a male, "to pieces" quite seriously. The younger dog is very submissive to her at most times other than play. She would certainly be ranked as a number two dog in my pack and was an alpha in this family unit. Every time the owners would yell at the male, the female would enforce her owners' words by attacking him to the point of bodily injury; several times they had to have these injuries surgically repaired at great expense. When she attacked him, he would immediately subdue himself to her. The cars, the owner's bed, the nighttime crates were all things that she was possessive about. These were areas of frequent and dangerous attacks. What started out as a very dominant female violently putting a submissive male in his place, in a violent manner, turned into a game for her as well.

Up to this point, the owners had tried constantly to stop this awful behavior. One owner even received a hand injury from trying to separate the female from the male. It was then that I met the lovely owners and started my work. After a dozen sessions with the dogs, I placed the female dog into the fire, and all I got was a look from her that said, "I would tear him apart if you were not here!" As the sessions rolled on "the look" said, "I know what I am not supposed to do, so can we please do something else?" At the conclusion of our time working together, fifty sessions over nine months, I never really got to correct the female for attacking the male in at least twenty hours of *encouraging her aggressive behavior* because she respected my handling from day one.

I am always amazed as to how much respect means to a dog, when properly taught. The dog must be given ideal guidance from the start of a working relationship. The owners started from below sea level and ended up with a good amount of respect from the female dog in comparison to what they started with. Since I started working with them the male has not been to the vet once for any injuries. The nasty thoughts will always be in the female's head, but as long as *she thinks before she bites*, everyone will be happy. This training has allowed the male's personality to bloom to a new level, despite his still being aware of the female's thoughts; he knows that she understands what is acceptable and what is not.

I have other stories like this one. What I hope you take from this story is that serious problems of this type can be resolved, but they take commitment and time. Many times, aggressive dogs need to be removed from the home, but if you can find a good dog trainer that has good communication skills with the dogs, then perhaps your beloved dog can be saved. The female dog in the story is a very trustworthy companion—however, be careful how much trust you give aggressive dogs!

Based on My Experience: Only Trust a Dog When You Have To!

My companion dog means as much to me as anything in this world, and I trust her with my life, but not with my "little" family members! I find that people trust and not trust their dogs in situations that are complete opposite of what they should! Hazel, my loyal companion dog, is a fabulous tracker. I have relied on her more times than I would have cared to in some of our adventures. If you do not have alternatives, and your dog can do something for you, let the dog do it! This same dog, which is as happy as any dog could possibly be, and loves to play fetch with anyone, including little kids... I do not trust around them. She has *never* displayed any aggression toward any person in her home, there is no reason to put the dog into a situation in an unsupervised environment where she could feel defensive or offensive. The consequences of trusting your dog alone with small children are too grave to test even the most gentle and trustworthy of dogs. Every dog can be made to feel uncomfortable and that can create a dangerous environment. So, please weigh this heavily before you run over to your neighbor's house for just a minute, leaving the children alone with even the most placid of dogs. The dog can do nothing wrong and the child can still get hurt. These conservative recommendations only come from experience.

Based on My Experience: The Curled-Tail Syndrome

I have created a theory based on my experiences with curled-tail dogs. They are neither naturally obedient nor trustworthy dogs. Asian breeds and Artic breeds often fall into this group of dogs. The number of curled-tail dogs that I could trust off leash have been few and far between. Many of these canines I feel are just very in touch with their wild side and that greatly affects their level of obedience. These dogs can rival any noncurled-tail dog at "on leash" obedience; however, when the freedom stick is removed, these dogs like to celebrate their liberties a bit more than most.

I get many calls on curled-tail dogs that have running problems. The twenty percent of dogs that I have had difficulty boundary training certainly includes a large number of dogs in this group. These dogs can make good companions, but they are usually dogs that a person cannot trust off leash. The classic buddy kind of dog is not usually in this group. These dogs have their moments when they act needy, but often they are aloof and independent. When these dogs are in a pack, they very seldom try to suck up attention. They will usually hang out with their pack members. Many of the artic breeds have nearly endless amounts of energy, and ninety-nine percent of the time they do not get enough exercise, which can lead to a certain level of neurosis. These dogs are often caged up because of their lack of obedience, and it can greatly affect their mental state. Due to being in touch with their wild side, it is not uncommon for these dogs to be aggressive creatures, especially when provoked, living in a human world, with human restraints being applied emotionally and physically. Unless you work with one of these breeds and are experienced with them, I would try to avoid bringing curled-tail dogs in your life.

Based on My Experience: Being Road Smart

When walking a dog on the road, I always stay on the left side. I create a walkway for the dog. First comes the shoulder of the road, then the canine, and then the handler. I normally walk with the dog on the road as opposed to the shoulder so the dog can heel well. Sometimes dogs have trouble heeling well on the shoulder of the road because of stones, sticks, etc. I usually stop when cars pass by, and place the dog on a "sit-stay." If a loud vehicle passes by and scares the canine, it might try to move quickly. If the dog is on the right side of the road, it will most likely move into the road because the handler is in between the dog and the shoulder of the road. If on the left side of the road and the dog gets scared it will most likely pull to the shoulder since the handler's body is blocking the dog from the road. The very nightmare that walking on the left reduces has unfortunately happened to several dogs. *Walk on the left please.*

Based on My Experience: Toss the Tie-Out!

I do not like to put a dog in a cage, but if the two choices were to place a dog in a kennel or tie-out a dog on a cable, I would choose the kennel. It is safer than a cable tie-out. A canine cannot hurt itself in a kennel, other than with very seldom cage biting. Nothing from the outside can hurt him or her because it cannot get into the kennel. Twice I have received phone calls from people telling me about the tragic loss of their dog due to being on a tie-out. Neither story is pleasant, but I am sharing this information to absolutely discourage you from using any tie-out apparatus. Thunderstorms, stray dogs, bees, tight collars, and other things can be extremely dangerous to your dog, especially while on a tie-out. Every time I work with dogs that are put out on a cable regularly, I call to tell the owners about these dangerous things and most of the time I have persuaded them to get a kennel.

Based on My Experience: Listen to What Others Have to Say

In terms of being not only a better teacher of dogs but a better person as well, it is very important to at least *listen* to everything anyone has to say. Well, this story is an example of my occasionally poor listening skills. I was on a seven-state road trip with all my dogs, in the summer of 2001. I had a goal to have Hazel swim in every state that we went to. I went from New York to Kentucky and bounced around in between. On our way home, we came up the coast. I stopped at Virginia Beach. After I went swimming, I found a place where we could take Hazel for a swim. I was on one of the channels of Chesapeake Bay. I am an inland, fresh-water kind of guy. The person who I was with grew up in the Caribbean and has been around oceans her whole life. Well, I was tossing a retrieving dummy for Hazel out into the channel and she was fetching it. She told me not to throw it so far out because the center current goes out into the ocean. I told her that I knew what I was doing. Well, two or three throws later finds me running a quarter to third of a mile down the shore screaming to Hazel as she swims about thirty miles per hour with the current, chasing the dummy out toward the ocean. Finally, several hundred feet later, Hazel got out of the current and swam safely to shore. That got the adrenaline pumping! There were a few "I told you so's" on that day! Please hear everyone out. I usually do, but I almost paid dearly for not listening that time. To this day I wonder what happened to that dummy…it was a real nice one.

Boundary Training: Bound to Travel

Canine Instinct's first official client was an owner who had a Dalmatian mix. This dog broke me in very well. She handled beautifully on lead, but off lead she was hell on wheels and then some! She loved to taunt me when she learned that I did not have control of her environment. After working with hundreds of dogs and then trying to start a real business, this dog scared me a little. But as time went on I realized that she was a special case, and as I began charging for my services this meant that many of my dogs were more than likely than not to have problems—and she did! She was under a year of age but she was thicker than any prison's walls!

The majority of canines can be taught to respect boundaries made by the handler; however, there are canines that are hopeless: mature dogs that have had no boundary training growing up, males, curled-tail dogs, and many hounds that I have experienced to be *travelers*, as I call them. At times, being a responsible owner of a canine means accepting the fact that you may not be capable of limiting your dog's boundaries without a physical barrier of some sort. Commonly, I receive calls from people who have only traveling problems with their dogs. A noteworthy percentage of the time these dogs refuse to comply with their owners' demands in this very important area. What follows are two more brief stories about some travelers that I have worked with.

The most comical traveler was a beagle mix about

three years old. The owners had rescued him from his previous home. He had always been tied up and had received little attention. His new owners were concerned about his wandering issues, as well as his lack of knowledge and respect for some basic commands.

This dog lived in a very urban area of town, and it was very dangerous for him to be gallivanting about the neighborhood. He would stay out for hours or sometimes not even come back home! Very close to his new home was a Super Kmart that the dog would go down to the store and visit the SuperK staff. This canine walked right into the store and met everyone. He was a regular! One of the managers would call the owners to let them know that their dog was there visiting again.

Toward the latter part of his training program, the dog had reduced his traveling to as little as ten to twenty minutes, and then returned home. Having the dog remain on the property without putting up a physical barrier seemed an impossibility. The dog was good with the majority of his basic obedience commands—he just had to do his thing.

The other traveler was a two-year-old husky that only had one-way tickets. He was amazing with "on leash" obedience, but once he was off leash he was gone in three seconds. He would be found miles away, on a regular basis. Sadly, the owner of chickens that this dog had been killing one by one over several weeks shot this husky. The chickens were over two miles from the husky's house. People between the dog's home and the chickens' residence would call the owners and inform them of their dog's unwelcome presence.

I think that for an owner this is one of the worst types of dogs that one can own and one of the worst kind of owners a dog can have. It is important for a trainer to work with these dogs because it keeps the trainers' teaching methods realistic; once you work with one of these guys, any feeling of imagined invincible communication powers vanish, as though you never had them. So please, to those working with these dogs, do not be as thickheaded as your four-legged student—it might not work!

Tracking: The Never-Ending Track

I taught a coonhound mix to do some basic tracking for fun back in 1998. This was the first time I had the owner set up the track for his dog. We were using gloves as the dog's reward upon discovery at the end of the track. This dog was tracking very well for me, and I felt confident that it would track the same for the owner. The owner made a track, almost oval-shaped. The owner sent the dog on the track and away she went! That canine worked her butt off for a good ten minutes. The dog seemed to be right on the trail the entire time. This track should have taken less than two minutes. She kept running the entire track, in an oval-shaped pattern. After ten minutes went by, I asked my client approximately where he dropped the glove. He looked at his hands and realized that he had both of his gloves on. He was so embarrassed. He told me that he was so nervous making the track all by himself that he forgot to drop a glove. So for ten minutes the canine made a big loop several times, looking at the owner like he was crazy. There was no reward out there for the canine to find. Let this be a lesson to make sure that there is always a reward on the track and that the canine finds it, if not by itself, then with the handler's help. Focus on the task at hand and try not to be nervous. If your tracker is doing circles for a while then check both hands to make sure that you are only wearing one glove.

Tracking: Nose over Navigator

It was December 2002, and there was over a foot of snow on the ground in the Central Adirondack region. My friend, Jasen, and I ventured out on our first snowshoe hike of the season. We both were all geared up and ready for nature's worst. At this time, I had owned a handheld personal navigator for about a year both to play around with and for safety concerns. Of course, Hazel was along for the trip as always.

Our snowshoe traveling had been about four miles in, close to two hours, up and down a few very rough inclines and declines, on this hike. We were just returning to our vehicle at dark. As we were unloading our gear into the car, I went to take my navigator off my belt, and discovered that it was not there! My heart rose into my throat and I could not breathe. My state-of-the-art four hundred dollar apparatus was somewhere in the wilderness. We were snowshoeing on familiar land so I did not use it at all. The navigator could have been anywhere along the way. Now it was pitch dark, and my navigator was missing in its black case in the woods. Jasen and I grabbed a flashlight and headed back into the forest.

I had been teaching Hazel to track for ten months and she was very advanced at this point. I guess this was the moment that she had been waiting for to shine. I sent her on a track ahead of us. About forty-five minutes later, Hazel comes to the heel position and hands me my navigator! She had a forty-five minute track in over a foot of snow, in the dark, in the Adirondacks, after an entire day of off and on snowshoeing. To top things off, it was her first track ever in the dark! It could have just been me, but when my loyal hardworking companion brought back my gadget, she seemed more proud than ever before. I am not sure if it was because this track was her most difficult ever or her way of saying that her nose is the only navigator I need. It was another exciting day that ended with a smile on my face and Hazel getting a big hug.

Duck Search Work: Duck or Dr. Pepper?

To watch a dog that has a desire to succeed and work often will bring happy tears to my eyes. Back in 1999, I was teaching a German shorthaired pointer to be a versatile hunter. This was a magnificent canine. Towards the completion of its training, I brought the dog to a pond in my area that was fairly vegetated with lily pads and with some old tree trunks laying in some shallow areas of the pond. This pond was probably a good five to eight acres in total size. I had driven down to the pond about two hours prior to our session and planted a duck dummy in a bundle of reeds about seventy feet or so from shore.

When the dog arrived, I fired a blank shot over the pond and sent the dog on a fetch. The dog worked as hard as any canine possibly could work for over twenty-five minutes. I threw two other dummies out, but she knew that those were not what I intended her to retrieve. I started to become concerned; not only was her search getting very long, but swimming in all of the vegetation had to be exceedingly difficult. She searched every single inch of that pond, including the reeds where I put the duck dummy. After thirty minutes she slowly pulled herself out of the water and came to me with her head down holding something. Hoping for approval, she had brought me an old Dr. Pepper soda can. She felt she had failed and she never had before. I picked up her head and gave her a kiss. With my eyes all glassy, I looked at my tired teammate and said, "I could not be any more proud of you." What a dog! What a search! What a scare!

Other than this being just another amazing dog story, you should know that when I went back out in the canoe to get the dummy, it was not there. I felt terribly guilty. I would imagine that a hawk took it, but the point here is to not plant dummies in the water two hours in advance. I let the dog down; she did not let me down.

Upland Hunting: They Can't Reason! Or Can They?

One of the most impressive things that I ever saw a canine do was to analyze a hunting episode. My client, his yellow lab, and I were duck hunting in mid-October on a creek. This creek has a series of small waterfalls about two hundred feet downstream from where we had our blind posted. We had taken a row-boat out to an island only about fifteen feet off shore. From one side to the other the creek was about sixty feet wide.

We sat patiently for a good forty minutes, and then at least a dozen ducks came overhead. My client shot once and dropped two ducks out of the sky. Both ducks landed in the water probably less than fifty feet away from us. He sent his lab for the retrieve, and the dog swam straight out to the ducks like a champ. He did not want to leave one behind, but he quickly came to terms with that and swam back to the island. My client sent him after the second duck. Before the dog went to complete his mission, he looked at the duck in the water, looked at the waterfalls, and then looked at the shore. He knocked me over and swam fifteen feet to shore, ran a good hundred-fifty feet downstream, and jumped in the water to get the duck before it went over the falls. Then he swam back to shore, ran up the stream, and swam back to the island.

Still to this day when I tell this story I would not believe it myself if I had not been there. *Impressed* is not even the word to describe what I felt. This is a great dog, but I did not think he was capable of pulling that one out of his sleeve! It just goes to show you what dogs can do when they have the desire to get the job done. He knew that there was no way he could get that duck in time if he swam straight out to it. I saw it in his eyes, when he looked at me to say, "Get out of my way because I am going to take the faster route." Desire brings out a canine's true potential and that potential has few limits.

Upland Hunting: Check Again Stupid!

One time to trust your dog is when he or she is your versatile hunting companion. It is the only way the job will get done. When you work with your dog, you trust your dog. The worse thing that *should* happen is that you are in the same circumstances as before you needed the canine's help. There are many stories I could tell using this story line, but the one I have chosen takes the cake. I taught a male German shorthaired pointer back in 2000 that has every right to call me stupid.

Now, I am always preaching *the nose knows*. Well... after forty minutes of searching for a bird, this dog was still rock solid on point. He slammed on point about an hour before dark, on a cold November day. He was pointing straight into the wind at a stone wall that was about six to eight feet in front of him. We were in an old, overgrown hay field. I thoroughly checked the brush, the knocked-down hay grass, and the stone wall. I tried to send him ahead to see if it was a false point or to repoint, but he would not budge. I fired a shot to see if he would go ahead and search...nope! I turned that piece of earth upside down. It looked like two bears had been rolling around.

After a half hour I was getting frustrated. I put my gun down on the ground and searched more vigorously. Forty minutes had gone by and I had broken into a cold sweat. There was one tree next to the stone wall where I was looking for the bird. As I went to hang my jacket on a lower branch, a quail that I had released earlier in the day flew out of a hole in the tree slightly above the dog's nose level. As the quail flew over the hill, I plopped down on the ground next to the dog and said, "Sorry buddy." He looked at me, as if saying, "Stupid human," then turned his head. So let me say it one more time, *the nose knows*.

Upland Hunting: A Bird Dog's Dream

My Hungarian Vizsla, Jake, and I went to a shooting preserve in the fall of 1997. This preserve released quail, chukars, and pheasants. We went for a half-day hunt. We started our hunt at around eight in the morning. About fifteen minutes later, Jake was rock solid on point and salivating profusely, to the point where I though he was having a seizure rather than being on point. I took a few steps in front of Jake, who was standing on top of a crest, and at least thirty or more quail took off from down below. It was like a mass of torpedoes going at the speed of light in every direction. I pulled one out to Jake's left. I told Jake to fetch and he remained like statue, in complete amazement. This was the only time to date that I have ever seen a dog salivate on point as a result of being overwhelmed by the amount of bird scent. But then again, I have never flushed thirty quail since that day either! About two minutes after the birds were flushed, Jake came back to life. He had no idea where the quail had fallen. It took him a few minutes to find it. Later, when we were returning to the truck, Jake stopped on that crest, and I think he played back the most wonderful surprise he had ever had in his life.

Upland Hunting: Pup versus Pheasant

Many bird hunters know that pheasants are not the best birds to bring up your pup on for several reasons. The main reason is because pheasants are serious runners. Especially for pointers, this is extremely bad because a runner entices the dog to chase. The other reason is because sometimes when the pup finds his or her bird, particularly a male pheasant, it might become a *fur-flying moment*. Male pheasants can get very aggressive and attack dogs from time to time. If the dog is young and/or sensitive, this can possibly ruin his or her hunting career.

I once trained a black lab for upland hunting. He is still a wonderful hunter, but he does have a fear. I worked with him when he was two years old. Three months into his training, hunting season had rolled around and we were working on state land, where pheasants are released every year. I was working this lab with pigeons at the time, and one day the dog discovered a big beautiful pheasant cock bird. The bird was less then five feet away from the lab when it took off running. It ran for a good hundred feet before running into a bush. Less than a minute later, the dog came out yelping. The cock bird had chased the lab for ten feet or so. The pheasant had pecked the dog in the eye. The injury warranted a visit to the vet. From that day on this black lab will not go into bushes anymore. Please be careful with your young dogs. I try to introduce pheasants as late as possible for this reason.

Upland Hunting: He Never Walks?

A few years back a friend of mine who had a German shorthaired pointer asked me if he and his dog could join Jake, my Vizsla, and I on a hunt during the second weekend in October. He had taught his dog—I had nothing to do with its training. His dog was two years old and Jake was five months older.

We met at the hunting grounds on Saturday morning. My friend asked me where were the birds that we were going to release. I had released three pheasants the evening before the hunt, over a half-mile area. He was a little upset about our bird scenario. We started our hunt. The dogs looked great. They both started out like champs. I told my friend that I was impressed. His dog was working as well as Jake.

The first half hour rolled by and there were no birds yet. Jake was working like a slave and my friend's dog was moping along behind us. My friend was getting upset with his dog. I had already realized why he was not enthusiastic. Early on in my career, I had made the same mistake many times with my hunting students. His dog was always rewarded too easily. I asked him how many birds he usually plants on each hunt when he is by himself with his dog. He replied confidently by stating two to five. He asked me the same question. I said zero to two, on the average hunt. His dog had lost its work ethic because it was not rewarded with a bird after only thirty minutes of hunting.

Considering this breed of dog, he should be equal with Jake in these skills, competing for the first find. The German shorthaired pointer did get a little spunk back after Jake pointed a bird, but never impressed me after the first half hour. Jake found two of the three pheas-ants in four hours that day; my buddy's dog thought it was the worst hunt ever! Always be sure that you make your dog earn his or her rewards when you are planting birds (or when doing other activities with your dog). A handler can under do it, but usually too many rewards with too little work creates a problem.

Upland Hunting: Admitting Defeat Brought Victory!

Once I taught a Brittany to hunt feather and fur. He was a great hunter. There was one problem; your hunt with him was going to be incredibly long! He knew that we were going to hunt for at least an hour or so. He would retrieve anything for a while, but once he thought that I would be bringing the hunt to an end he would stop retrieving to hand. I tried putting him on a long lead; he just stood there from day one with the lead on and said, "This stinks!" I would get a pheasant, and he would come within ten feet of me and drop it, then resume hunting. I would get a rabbit, and he would bring it within ten feet of me and drop it. This was truly a dog that lived to hunt.

After over four months of training, I discovered a way to get him to come to me so I could put the leash back on him. Believe me, I tried everything! It was not until I sat down in the woods on one of our hunts, after three hours, and said to myself, "This will be the first dog that I cannot get to comply with me." At this time, I was taking the dog into my home for training, so the owner had no influence on the dog in a negative sense while in training.

This Brittany was a team dog—he just did not want to stop the hunt. Well, when I sat down on the ground for an hour, the dog realized that he needed me just as much as I need him to complete our task. He stood and stared at me for nearly that entire hour before he came over to me and licked my face. I stroked his head, gave him some praise and continued to hunt. I was thrilled that he had come to me voluntarily and he was thrilled that we resumed hunting! Another hour later I sat down after we had just gotten a bird, and he brought it right to my lap. I am always saying that we need the dog to get the job done, and boy do we ever! But the dog needs us, too, this dog certainly learned that.

Upland Hunting: Trying Too Hard!

In the introduction of this book I mentioned my father's German shorthaired pointer, Jessie. What a dog! She was one of the most naturally gifted dogs I have ever hunted with. No one taught her a darn thing. She was all about natural ability.

I look back and often think of the days when I hunted with Jessie. At twelve years old I could go hunting with Jess, bag a few birds, have a happy dog, and have her listen to me when need be *in the field*. I always remember that because people try all these fancy, new, harsh, you-name-it-kind-of-things, and I think that all that does is complicate matters. So to this day, I try to do what I did when I was twelve: watch, learn, and help the dog get the job done. People are too aggressive when they want total control, and they want to know where and what the dog is going to do. They accomplish their goals most of the time, but the dog is being forced to use its abilities according to the handler. It might sound good, but these canines will not reach their potential, nor will the handler enjoy himself or herself as much. Some dogs do need tremendous amounts of work, but if the dog learns in a freestyle environment, the handler has little work to do. Setting up the ideal learning environment should be the focus for the handler. At twelve, my dog did as well as she did because I took her hunting a lot. I did nothing but encourage her "birdie" behavior, and she was an awesome dog. The harder one tries, the more room there is for error. Let things come as naturally as possible and encourage things gently that are slow in coming.

Special Thanks

For the past several years I have said to myself and to my clients that some day I am going to write a book. It takes a lot of desire, time, and confidence to make it happen. An old friend of mine who motivated me to put my knowledge on paper to share it with the public is Mario Picayo. I have had all the knowledge to write a book on teaching the canine for a few years now, but it might have never have come to be if it was not for Mario, who inspired and pushed me to make one of my dreams a reality. So thanks to Mario, that book that I had always talked about, you, my reader, are about to finish! Thank you Mario.

Elin Minkoff was a client of mine a couple of years ago, and we grew to become good friends. She volunteered to proofread my book and give me any help that she could. She has done that very thing. My book would have been tremendously more difficult without her, and she made the whole writing experience enjoyable. Thank you Elin.

A big thanks has to go out to all the people and to my

clients who have given me the delightful privilege of teaching their dog(s) in order to further my own education. Without all of you, Canine Instinct would not be what it is today. Thank you all.

Lastly, I have to thank all of my dogs. They are the ones that have motivated me to do as much as I do with them. They have been my *unconditional* friends through the bad times as well as the good times. My dogs are a true representation of what Canine Instinct is all about. It is about reaching their maximum potential and having a heck of a good time getting there!

In Loving Memory Of Jake

Jake was my dearest friend and companion that had shared the best of times and the worst of times with me. Jake is a dog that contributed to who I am today. His regal, suave, and charming personality placed him in the deepest part of everyone's heart. My methods are based upon love, respect, and trust; Jake represents just those essential elements in life. He made me a better person, teacher, handler, and most importantly friend. Truthfully, Jake is the one of the leading factors that has brought Canine Instinct to where it is today. I am grateful for the opportunity to have worked with one of the finest canines that I have ever known. I always tell people that dogs are good at making people feel important. Well, Jake had mastered this art and I want him to know that he was needed as much in every way that he felt I was needed. I dedicate this book to the best friend I have ever had. Rest in peace, my friend, I love you.

Jake

Stay. Come. Heel. Every Time.

Printed in the United States
46829LVS00002B/172-468

9 781595 409348